Much Ado About Nothing

莎翁戏剧经典

无事生非

〔英〕威廉·莎士比亚 著

申恩荣 注释

商务印书馆
The Commercial Press
SINCE 1897

2016 年·北京

威廉·莎士比亚

图 1

图 2（见 4 页）

In front of Leonato's house
Enter Leonato, Governor of Messina, Hero his daughter,
and Beatrice his niece, with a Messenger.
LEONATO
I learn in this letter that Don Pedro of Arragon
Comes this night to Messina.
MESSENGER He is very near by this. He was not three
Leagues off when I left him.

图 3 （见 10 页）

BENEDICK　What，my dear Lady Disdain! Are you yet living?
BEATRICE　Is it possible Disdain should die while she
hath such meet food to feed it as Signior Benedick?
Courtesy itself must convert to Disdain if you come in
her presence.

图 4（见 20 页）

CLAUDIO

Hath Leonato any son, my lord?

PEDRO

No child but Hero; she's his only heir.

Dost thou affect her, Claudio?

图 5（见 30 页）

CONRADE To the death, my lord.

JOHN Let us to the great supper. Their cheer is the greater that I am subdued. Would the cook were o' my mind! Shall we go prove what's to be done?

图 6（见 32 页）

The hall of Leonato's house
Enter Leonato, his brother [Antonio],
Hero his daughter, and Beatrice his niece
[also Margaret and Ursula].

LEONATO Was not Count John here at supper?

ANTONIO I saw him not.

BEATRICE How tartly that gentleman looks! I never can
See him but I am heart-burned an hour after.

图 7（见 56 页）

Enter [Don] John and Borachio.

JOHN It is so. The Count Claudio shall marry the daughter
of Leonato.

BORACHIO Yea, my lord; but I can cross it.

JOHN Any bar, any cross, any impediment will be medicinable
to me.

图 8（见 68 页）

LEONATO O, when she had writ it, and was reading it over, she found 'Benedick' and 'Beatrice' between the sheet?

CLAUDIO That.

LEONATO O, she tore the letter into a thousand half-pence, railed at herself that she should be so immodest to write to one that she knew would flout her. 'I measure him,' says she, 'by my own spirit; for I should flout him if he writ to me. Yea, though I love him, I should.'

图 9（见 76 页）

Leonato's orchard

Enter Hero and two Gentlewomen, Margaret and Ursula.

HERO

Good Margaret, run thee to the parlor.

There shalt thou find my cousin Beatrice

Proposing with the Prince and Claudio.

Whisper her ear and tell her, I and Ursula

Walk in the orchard, and our whole discourse

Is all of her. ...

图 10（见 84 页）

BEATRICE [*coming forth from hiding*]
What fire is in mine ears? Can this be true?
Stand I condemned for pride and scorn so much?
Contempt, farewell! And maiden pride, adieu!
No glory lives behind the back of such.
And, Benedick, love on; I will requite thee,
Taming my wild heart to thy loving hand.

图 11（见 92 页）

A street in Messina
Enter Dogberry and his compartner [Verges],
with the Watch .

DOGBERRY Are you good men and true?

VERGES Yea, or else it were pity but they should suffer
salvation, body and soul.

DOGBERRY Nay, that were a punishment too good for
them if they should have any allegiance in them, being
chosen for the Prince's watch.

图 12（见 98 页）

2. WATCH Well, masters, we hear our charge. Let us go sit
here upon the church bench till two, and then all to bed.

DOGBERRY One word more, honest neighbors. I pray you
watch about Signior Leonato's door, for the wedding
being there to-morrow, there is a great coil to-night.
Adieu. Be vigitant, I beseech you.

     Exeunt [*Dogberry and Verges*].
  Enter Borachio and Conrade.

图 13（见 112 页）

VERGES And we must do it wisely.

DOGBERRY We will spare for no wit, I warrant you.
Here's that shall drive some of them to a non-come.
Only get the learned writer to set down our excommunication,
and meet me at the jail.   [*Exeunt.*]

图 14（见 114 页）

Within a Church in Messina
Enter Prince [Don Pedro], [John the] Bastard, Leonato,
  Friar [Francis], Claudio, Benedick, Hero, and Beatrice
  [and Attendants].

LEONATO Come, Friar Francis, be brief. Only to the
plain form of marriage, and you shall recount their
particular duties afterwards.

FRIAR You come hither, my lord, to marry this lady?

CLAUDIO No.

图 15（见 134 页）

BENEDICK By my sword, Beatrice, thou lovest me.

BEATRICE Do not swear and eat it.

BENEDICK I will swear by it that you love me, and I will make him eat it that says I love not you.

BEATRICE Will you not eat your word?

图 16（见 138—140 页）

A hearing-room in Messina
Enter the Constables [Dogberry and Verges]
And the Town Clerk [Sexton] in gowns, Borachio,
[Conrade, and Watch].

...

    1. WATCH This man said, sir, that Don John
      the Prince's brother was a villain.
DOGBERRY Write down Prince John a villain. Why, this
is flat perjury, to call a prince's brother villain.
BORACHIO Master constable —

图 17（见 142 页）

CONRADE Away! you are an ass，you are an ass.
DOGBERRY Dost thou not suspect my place? Dost thou
not suspect my years? O that he were here to write me
down an ass! But，masters，remember that I am an
ass. Though it be not written down，yet forget not
that I am an ass. ...

图 18 (见 144 页)

A Street in Messina
Enter Leonato and his brother [Antonio].

ANTONIO

If you go on thus, you will kill yourself,
And 'tis not wisdom thus to second grief
Against yourself.

LEONATO I pray thee cease thy counsel,
Which falls into mine ears as profitless
As water in a sieve. ...

图 19 (见 158 页)

CLAUDIO Hearken after their offense, my lord.

PEDRO Officers, what offense have these men done?

DOGBERRY Marry, sir, they have committed false report;
moreover, they have spoken untruths; secondarily,
they are slanders; sixth and lastly, they have belied
a lady; thirdly, they have verified unjust things; and to
conclude, they are lying knaves.

图 20（见 166 页）

In front of Leonato's house

Enter Benedick and Margaret [*meeting*].

BENEDICK Pray thee, sweet Mistress Margaret, deserve
well at my hands by helping me to the speech of Beatrice.

MARGARET Will you then write me a sonnet in praise of
my beauty?

图 21（见 174 页）

A Churchyard
Enter Claudio, Prince [Don Pedro, Lord],
And three or four with tapers [followed
by musicians].

CLAUDIO Is this the monument of Leonato?

LORD It is, my lord.

CLAUDIO [*reads from a scroll*]
    Epitaph.
   Done to death by slanderous tongues
    Was the Hero that here lies.
   Death, in guerdon of her wrongs,
    Gives her fame which never dies.
   So the life that died with shame
   Lives in death with glorious fame.
    [*Hangs up the scroll.*]
   Hang thou there upon the tomb,
   Praising her when I am dumb.
Now, music, sound, and sing your solemn hymn.

图 22（见 182 页）

LEONATO

No，that you shall not till you take her hand
Before this friar and swear to marry her.

CLAUDIO

Give me your hand before this holy friar.
I am your husband if you like of me.

HERO

And when I lived I was your other wife；
[*Unmasks*]
And when you loved you were my other husband.

图 23（见 186 页）

MESSENGER
My lord，your brother John is ta'en in flight，
And brought with armed men back to Messina.
BENEDICK   Think not on him till to-morrow. I'll devise
thee brave punishments for him. ...

"莎翁戏剧经典"丛书总序

  莎士比亚(William Shakespeare，1564－1616)是英国 16 世纪文艺复兴时期的伟大剧作家和诗人，也是世界文坛上的巨擘。他一生创作了 38 部戏剧作品(一说 37 部)，诗作包括两部长篇叙事诗、一部十四行诗集以及其他一些短篇诗作。四百多年来这些作品被翻译成多种文字，在世界各地广泛传播。正如他同时代的批评家和剧作家本·琼生所说，他是"时代的灵魂"，"不属一个时代，而属于所有的时代!"莎士比亚在世期间，他的戏剧作品曾吸引了大量观众，包括宫廷王室成员和普通百姓，产生了巨大影响。18 世纪以来，这些作品始终活跃在舞台上，20 世纪随着电影业的发展，它们又被搬上银幕。几百年来，无论是体现莎士比亚原作的表演还是经过不断改编的作品，莎剧都拥有众多的观者，散发出不灭的艺术光辉;另一方面，自 1623 年莎士比亚全集第一对开本问世，莎士比亚的戏剧也成为学者和广大普通读者阅读、学习、研究的对象，在历代读者的阅读和研究中，这些作品不断得到新阐释和挖掘。莎士比亚的作品焕发着永久不衰的生命活力。

  1564 年 4 月，莎士比亚出生于英格兰中部的埃文河畔的斯特拉福镇。家境殷实，父亲曾经营手套和羊毛，并做过小镇的镇长。莎士比亚小时曾在镇上的文法学校读书，受到过较为正规的拉丁文和古典文学的教育。不久，家道中落，陷入经济困境，这可能成为莎士比亚后来未能进入大学读书的原因。1582 年，莎士比亚十八岁时与邻村一位大他八岁的女子安·哈撒韦成婚，六个月后，大女儿苏珊娜降生，此后他们又有了一对孪生子女，不幸的是，儿子哈姆内特早夭。16 世纪 90 年代左右，莎士比亚来到伦敦，发展他的戏剧事业。他曾是剧团的演员、编剧和股东。90 年代初期，莎士比亚即开始戏剧创作。1592 年，莎士比亚已在同行中崭露头角，被当时的"大学才子"剧作家格林所嫉妒，他把莎士比亚称作"那只新抖起来的乌鸦"，"借我们的羽毛来打扮自己……狂妄地幻想着能独自震撼（Shake-scene）这个国家的舞台"。1592—1594 年间，伦敦因流行瘟疫，大部分剧院关闭，在此期间莎士比亚完成了两部著名的长篇叙事诗《维纳斯与阿多尼斯》与《鲁克丽丝受辱记》。1594 年剧院恢复营业之后，莎士比亚加入宫廷大臣剧团，并终生服务于该剧团，直到 1613 年离开伦敦返回家乡。90 年代中期，他进入了戏剧创作的巅峰时期。在 1590 年至 1613 年的二十多年之间，莎士比亚共创作了历史剧、悲剧、喜剧、传奇剧等 38 部。90 年代中后期，他的创作以喜剧和历史剧为主，包括喜剧《仲夏夜之梦》(1595)、《威尼斯商人》(1596)、《无事生非》(1598—1599)、《皆大欢喜》(1599—1600)等和大部分历史剧，如《理查三世》(1592—1593)、《亨利四世》（上、下）(1596—1598)、《亨利五世》(1598—1599)等。这一时期，他的创作风格较为明快，充满积极向上的格调，即便剧中有悲剧的成分，整个作品也透露出对生活的肯定，对理想的向往，如《罗密欧与朱丽叶》(1595)。进入 17 世纪后，莎士比亚的戏剧更多地转向对人生重大问题的思考，探索解决人生之困顿的途径，诸如权力、欲望、嫉妒、暴政等等。四大悲剧《哈姆莱特》(1600—1601)、《奥瑟罗》(1603—1604)、《李尔王》(1605—1606)、《麦克白》(1606)均完成于这一时期。此外，几部重要的罗马题材剧也在 90 年代末和新世纪的最初几年完成，如《裘力·凯撒》(1599)、《安东尼与克里奥佩特拉》(1606)、《科里奥兰纳斯》(1608)等。莎士比亚这一时期也创作了几部喜剧，但风格较前一时期更多悲情色彩，更为沉重而引人深思。1609 年，莎士比亚《十四行诗集》出版。晚期的莎士比亚剧作风格有一定变化，最有影响的是传奇剧，如《暴风雨》，通过想象的世界与现实世界的对照来探讨人生问题。

　　莎士比亚的名字开始传入中国是在 19 世纪中上叶，他的戏剧被翻译成汉语而为国人所知则是在 20 世纪初期。当时，他剧作的内容通过英国 19 世纪兰姆姐弟《莎士比亚戏剧故事集》的汉译被介绍到中国来,即无译者署名的《澥外奇谭》(1903)和林纾、魏易翻译的《吟边燕语》(1904)。20世纪20年代,莎剧汉译事业的开拓者田汉翻译了《哈孟雷特》(1921)和《罗密欧与朱丽叶》(1924)。此后,朱生豪、梁实秋、孙大雨、曹禺、曹未风、虞尔昌等译家都翻译过莎士比亚的剧作。朱生豪先生在经历日本侵略的苦难、贫穷和疾病折磨的极其艰苦的环境下,以惊人的毅力和顽强的意志,克服种种艰难险阻,穷毕生之精力完成了31部半莎剧的翻译,成为播撒莎士比亚文明之火的普罗米修斯,译莎事业的英雄和圣徒。他的莎剧译文优美畅达,人物性格鲜明,成为广大读者所珍爱的艺术瑰宝。梁实秋是中国迄今为止唯一一位个人独立完成莎剧和莎诗汉译工程的翻译家。梁译有详尽的注释和说明,学术含量较高。1956年,卞之琳翻译的《哈姆雷特》出版,他完善了孙大雨提出的翻译原则,提出"以顿代步、韵式依原诗、等行翻译"的翻译方法,可谓开一代诗体译法之风,他的译本至今都被视作该剧最优秀的译本。方平是另一位重要的成绩卓著的莎剧翻译家。2000年由他主编主译的《新莎士比亚全集》出版,其中25部莎剧由方平翻译,其他作品由阮坤、吴兴华、汪义群、覃学岚、屠岸、张冲等译出,为国内目前首部全部由分行诗体翻译的莎剧莎诗全集。

时至今日,莎士比亚的戏剧作品仍不断有新的译本出版,对广大读者而言,阅读汉译的莎剧已经是一件十分方便的事情,而这些汉译莎剧作品中不乏优秀的译本。然而,尽管莎剧的汉译丰富多彩,莎剧的改编层出不穷,要想真正了解莎剧的本来面目,我们还须要回到莎剧原文本身。其中的原因有三:一、每一种语言都是丰富的,其表达的意义可能是多元多面的,但由于译出语和译入语两种语言之间的差异,再好的翻译也只能尽可能地贴近原文而不可能百分之百地再现原文的魅力,因此,阅读再好的译本也无法取代或等同于阅读原作;二、莎士比亚生活的时代距今已经有约400年,他所使用的英语与今天人们所熟悉的英语已有较大差异,当时的人们所熟悉的文化和历史事件也是我们今天并不熟知的,因此,要真正领悟他的作品,还须回到他那时的语言和文化中去；三、莎剧经过约 400 年的变迁，在改编中不断变换，有些已经走出了莎士比亚时代的莎剧，因而，想要认识和了解莎剧，最佳的办法还是回到莎剧的原文本中去。

莎士比亚生活和创作的时期在 16 世纪末 17 世纪初。英语在当时已经得到极大的发展，十分活跃而成熟，尤其莎士比亚戏剧中所运用的英语，文辞丰富、结构灵活、表达力很强。但随着时代的发展，其中的一些用词、用语以及语义等都发生了变化，与我们今天的英语存在一定距离，理解起来也就会有一定困难。莎剧在绝大多数情况下采用的是诗体写作，即人物的语言是分行的，每行十个音节，轻重音节相间，一轻一重的每两个音节构成一个音步，不押韵，因此，他的剧作均为抑扬格五音步的素体诗。这样的诗体形式突显出莎剧语言的艺术魅力，音韵优美、铿锵，节奏感强，表达生动有力。然而，正因为这是诗体写作，在语法上就可能出现诗语言特有的结构，比如倒装句或词序颠倒的现象等。莎剧的语言丰富多彩，不同人物的话语呈现出多种特色，时而体现出古典拉丁语的文风，时而出现双关语、俚语、隐喻等修辞手法。典故、历史事件、政治元素、宗教、生活习俗等等都可能成为今天的读者理解莎剧原文本的障碍。因而，借助良好的注释来理解莎剧的原作就成为我们了解和认识莎剧原貌的必要手段。这次由商务印书馆隆重推出的"莎翁戏剧经典"丛书，重点选出莎士比亚的 12 部经典剧作，在裘克安先生主编的"莎士比亚注释"丛书的基础上进行了改编修订，并加入了精美的插图。裘先生主编的"莎士比亚注释"丛书对莎剧原文做了多方面的详尽注释，对理解原文起到有效作用，在读者中有较广泛的影响。相信这套"莎翁戏剧经典"的出版会进一步推动莎剧在广大读者中的影响力，提高人们对阅读莎剧以及经典文学作品原文的兴趣和能力，产生积极的和广泛的影响。

屠岸 章燕

2013 年 10 月 4 日

"莎士比亚注释"丛书总序

莎士比亚研究在新中国有过不平坦的道路和坎坷的命运。解放后不久,大家纷纷学俄语,学英语的人数骤减。研究英国文学,要看苏联人怎么说。"文革"十年,莎士比亚同其他西方"资产阶级"作家一样被打入冷宫。改革开放以后,1978年人民文学出版社出版了在朱生豪译文基础上修订补足的《莎士比亚全集》。随之又出版了一些个别剧的不同译本,如方平译的《莎士比亚喜剧五种》(1979年)和卞之琳译的《莎士比亚悲剧四种》(1988年)。梁实秋的译本,现在大陆上也可以读到了。评介和研究莎士比亚的文章,从"文革"结束后才逐渐多起来。

但是,目前多数人学习、欣赏和研究莎士比亚,是通过中译文来进行的。精通英语而研究莎士比亚的学者不是没有,然而他们人数不多,年纪却老迈了。最近若干年,才有一些年轻人到英国或美国去学习和研究莎士比亚。

1981年我就想到有必要在中国出版我们自己注释的莎士比亚著作。谈起来,许多朋友都赞成。1984年中国莎士比亚研究会筹备和成立时,我自告奋勇,联系了一些志同道合的学者,共同开始编写莎士比亚注释本。商务印书馆大力支持出版这套丛书。到2002年底已出书26种,而且第一次印刷版已全部售完。这证明这套丛书是很受欢迎的。

要知道,莎士比亚是英语文学中最优秀的代表人物,他又是英语语言大师,学习、欣赏和研究他的原著,是译文无法替代的。商务印书馆以其远见卓识,早在1910年和1921—1935年间,就出版过几种莎士比亚剧本的注释本,以满足这方面的需求。那时的教会学校学生英文水平高,能读莎著;不但大学生能读,连有些中学生都能读。可从那时以后,整整50年中国就没印过原文的莎士比亚著作。

世界各国，莎著的注释本多得不计其数。如果唯独中国没有，实在说不过去。如果没有，对于中国知识分子欣赏和研究莎士比亚十分不利。近年来，中国人学英语的越来越多了，他们的英文水平也逐渐提高了。因此，也存在着一定的读者市场。

有了注释本，可以为明天的莎士比亚研究提供一个可靠的群众基础。而译本显然不能提供可靠的基础。

莎士比亚是16、17世纪之交的作者，他写的又是诗剧。对于现代的读者，他的英语呈现着不少的困难。不要说掌握了现代英语的中国读者，就是受过一般教育的英美人士，在初读莎士比亚原著时也面临许多障碍，需要注释的帮助。

莎士比亚的时代，英语正从受屈折变化拘束的中世纪英语，向灵活而丰富的现代英语转变。拉丁语和法语当时对英语影响很大。而莎士比亚对英语的运用又有许多革新和创造。主要的困难可以归纳为以下几个方面，也就是注释要提供帮助的方面：

（一）词汇。许多词虽然拼法和现在一样，但具有不同的早期含义，不能望文生义。另有一些词拼法和现在不一样，而含义却相同。莎士比亚独创了一些词。他特别喜欢用双关语，在他创作的早期尤其如此。而双关语是无从翻译的。这是译本无论如何也代替不了注释本的原因之一。

让我们举《哈姆莱特》剧中男主角出场后最初讲的几句话为例：

> King：But now，my cousin Hamlet，and my son ——
> Hamlet〔Aside〕：A little more than kin，and less than kind!
> King：How is it that the clouds still hang on you?
> Hamlet：Not so，my lord. I am too much i' the sun.

· 梁实秋的译文如下：

> 王：现在，我的侄子哈姆雷特，也是我的儿子，——
> 哈〔旁白〕：比侄子是亲些，可是还算不得儿子。
> 王：怎么，你脸上还是罩着一层愁云？
> 哈：不是的，陛下；我受的阳光太多了。

· 卞之琳的译文如下：

王:得,哈姆雷特,我的侄子,我的儿——

哈[旁白]:亲上加亲,越亲越不相亲!

王:你怎么还是让愁云惨雾罩着你?

哈:陛下,太阳大,受不了这个热劲"儿"。

• 朱生豪的译文如下:

王:可是来,我的侄儿哈姆莱特,我的孩子——

哈[旁白]:超乎寻常的亲族,漠不相干的路人。

王:为什么愁云依旧笼罩在你的身上?

哈:不,陛下;我已经在太阳里晒得太久了。

这里,主要困难在于莎士比亚让哈姆莱特使用了 kin 和 kind 以及 son 和 sun 两组双关语。kind 一词又有双关意义,翻译无法完全表达,只能各译一个侧面。结果,梁和卞两先生还得用注释补足其义,朱译则连注释也没有。这种地方,能读原文注释本的人才能充分领略莎氏原意。

哈姆莱特在旁白里说:比亲戚多一点——本来我是你的侄子,现在又成了你的儿子,确实不是一般的亲戚关系啊;然而却比 kind 少一点——kind 有两层意思,一是"同类相求"的亲近感,一是"与人为善"的善意感,我同你没有共同语言,我也不知道你是安的什么心。这话只能对自己说,在舞台上假定对方是听不到的。哈姆莱特的第二句话是公开的俏皮话:哪里有什么阴云呀,我在太阳里晒得不行呢。sun 是跟 clouds 相对;太阳又意味着国王的恩宠,"你对我太好了,我怎么会阴郁呢?"sun 又跟 son 谐音,"做你的儿子,我领教得够了。"原文并不是像梁实秋所说的那样晦涩难解。可是含义太复杂,有隐藏的深层感情,所以无法译得完全。

(二)语法。有些现象,按现代英语语法的标准看,似乎是错误的,但在当时并不错,是属于中世纪英语的残余因素。例如有些动词过去分词的词尾变化、代词的所有格形式、主谓语数的不一致、关系代词和介词的用法等方面,都有一些和现在不同的情况。注释里说明了,可以举一反三去理解。

(三)词序的颠倒和穿插。词尾屈折变化较多的中世纪英语本来对词序没有严格的要求。伊丽莎白时代继承了这种习惯。同时，诗的节律和押韵要求对词序作一定的灵活处理。莎士比亚的舞台语言以鲜明、有力、生动为首要考虑，有时他就把语法和句法放在从属的地位。在激动的台词中，由于思路、感情的变化，语言也常有脱出常规的变化。这些地方，有了注释的指点，理解就容易得多。

（四）典故。莎士比亚用典很多。古希腊、罗马神话，《圣经》故事，英国民间传说，历史逸事……他都随手拈来。其中有一大部分对于英美读者来说乃是常识，但中国读者就很需要注释的帮助。

（五）文化背景。注释可以提供关于基督教义、中世纪传统观点、文艺复兴时期新的主张、英国习俗等方面的知识。

除上述以外，还有莎剧中影射时事，以及版本考据诸问题，在注释本中可以详细论述，也可以简单提及。

世界文豪莫不是语言大师，而要真正理解和欣赏一位大师的文笔，当然非读他的原著不成。出版莎士比亚注释本，首先是为了让中国读者便于买到和读到他的原著。不过我们自知现出的几十种在版本、注释和其他方面还存在不足之处，希望读者多提意见，以便今后不断改进。

裘克安

前　　言

　　威廉·莎士比亚1564年4月生于英国中部埃文河畔斯特拉福镇上一个相当富裕的市民家庭。他在镇上的文法学校念过书，主要读拉丁文，可能也读点希腊文。离开学校后，他曾帮助他父亲做过各种各样的生意，据说还当过乡间学校的助理教师。大约在1585年，他到了伦敦，在剧院里干些下等工作，后来当了演员，并开始了戏剧创作活动。起初改编别人的老剧本，然后转到独立创作。现在保存下来的37部剧本（一说38部），只不过是他在伦敦时期所写的剧本中的一部分。大约在1612年，他离开伦敦回到斯特拉福镇；1616年4月逝世，享年52岁。

　　莎士比亚是一个伟大的戏剧创作大师，同时又是一个完全掌握了诗的语言的天才诗人。马克思称道过，"莎士比亚的创作是世界艺术顶峰之一"。

　　《无事生非》是莎士比亚喜剧艺术达到成熟时期的一部作品，是其四大喜剧（《威尼斯商人》、《无事生非》、《皆大欢喜》、《第十二夜》）之一。剧本的主要故事是阿拉贡亲王庶弟唐·约翰企图破坏克劳狄奥和希罗的婚事，对他们进行诬陷，最后以失败告终；而实际上最吸引人的情节乃是另一对个性很强且嘴不饶人的青年男女培尼狄克和贝特丽丝，从互相抬杠到最后互诉爱慕。希罗受冤屈的故事系根据旧有的意大利小说，甚至是根据一本已失传的英国剧本；但贝特丽丝、培尼狄克和丑角道格培里等人物却是莎士比亚的伟大创造。莎士比亚四大喜剧中的四个女主角鲍西娅、贝特丽丝、罗瑟琳、薇奥拉各有其独特的风采和魅力，而贝特丽丝却是最真实可爱的，她为人直爽、活泼、乐观，谈锋犀利，才华过人。在她对希罗的友情中，显示了她的真挚和忠诚。她和培尼狄克的互不相让、唇枪舌剑的交锋，仿佛是一席机智才华的盛宴(a feast of wit),特别是她那心直口快、妙语连珠的风趣谈吐,令人喜爱倾倒,玩味无穷。贝特丽丝对培尼狄克的爱情并不是希罗和克劳狄奥等人巧计安排的结果,而是他们俩原来彼此都有好感。如在剧本开始时,我们就可以看出贝特丽丝对培尼狄克的关心。他们的爱情发展到不可抑制,意味着他们从各自的偏见中摆脱出来,性格上趋于成熟;他们的结合是建立在相互了解和感情的呼应上的。这个剧本的结尾是两对情人同时举行婚礼。

《无事生非》是一种"高尚的喜剧"(High Comedy),对话具有温文尔雅的性质,旨在诉诸人们的理智。它的文字亦韵亦散,绚丽多姿;语言丰富多彩,用词生动有力。剧本的主要人物都是受过教育的上层人士,他们惯于玩弄智力游戏和机智的反驳,谈话充满风趣,十分幽默和俏皮。另一些人物是下层社会没有受过什么教育的,如道格培里等。他们没有什么学问,而又故意装作有学问,在用词方面经常出现荒谬的错误。他们想方设法把话说得俏皮些,结果却令人捧腹大笑。莎士比亚真不愧是一位语言大师。

《无事生非》是莎士比亚约于1598年创作的。最早印本是根据莎士比亚所在剧团演出时的手抄脚本于1600年出版的第一版四开本。1623年又将它收入第一版对开合订本中。现代版本一般由版本专家对1600年和1623年两种版本进行研究和鉴定,互相对照补充,并将拼写和标点符号适当现代化。

在莎士比亚时代,他的所有出版了的剧本不分幕和场;由此可以推断莎士比亚的手写脚本也是不分幕和场的。但在1623年出版的对开合订本中,有的剧本分了幕和场,有的不分。现在已全部分了幕和场,注了行码。我们按照行码的顺序作了注释。本书的前言和注释承裘克安先生细心审校,作了一些修改,特在此表示衷心的感谢。

申恩荣

于湖南师范大学外语系

MUCH ADO ABOUT NOTHING

DRAMATIS PERSONAE

Don Pedro [dɔn 'piːdrəu], Prince of Arragon ['ærəgən]
Don John [dɔn dʒɔn], his bastard brother
Claudio ['klɔːdiəu], a young lord of Florence ['flɔrens]
Benedick ['benidik], a young lord of Padua ['pædjuə]
Leonato [li(ː)ə'naːtəu], Governor of Messina [me'siːnə]
Antonio [æn'təuniəu], an old man, his brother
Balthasar [ˌbælθə'zɑː], attendant of Don Pedro
Borachio [bə'rɑːtʃiəu] ⎱
Conrade ['kɔnreid] ⎰ followers of Don John
Friar Francis ['fraiə 'frɑːnsis]
Dogberry ['dɔgberi], a constable
Verges ['vəːdʒəz], a headborough
A Sexton ['sekstən]
Hero ['hiərəu], daughter to Leonato
Beatrice ['biətris], niece to Leonato
Margaret ['mɑːgərit] ⎱
Ursula ['əːsjulə] ⎰ waiting gentlewomen attending on Hero
Messengers, Watch, Lords, Attendants, Musicians, etc.
    Scene: Messina

注 释

唐·彼德罗,阿拉贡亲王
唐·约翰,他的庶弟
克劳狄奥
培尼狄克
里奥那托
安东尼奥
鲍尔萨泽
波拉契奥 }
康拉德 }
法兰西斯神父
道格培里
弗吉斯
教堂司事
希罗
贝特丽丝
玛格莱特 }
欧苏拉 }
梅西那

ACT I

SCENE I

In front of Leonato's house

*Enter Leonato, Governor of Messina, Hero his
daughter, and Beatrice his niece, with a Messenger.*

LEONATO I learn in this letter that Don Pedro of Arragon
comes this night to Messina.

MESSENGER He is very near by this. He was not three
leagues off when I left him.

5   LEONATO How many gentlemen have you lost in this
action?

MESSENGER But few of any sort, and none of name.

LEONATO A victory is twice itself when the achiever
brings home full numbers. I find here that Don Pedro

10   hath bestowed much honor on a young Florentine called
Claudio.

MESSENGER Much deserved on his part, and equally remembered by Don Pedro. He hath borne himself beyond
the promise of his age, doing in the figure of a lamb the
feats of a lion. He hath indeed better bettered

15   expectation than you must expect of me to tell you how.

LEONATO He hath an uncle here in Messina will be very
much glad of it.

MESSENGER I have already delivered him letters, and
there appears much joy in him; even so much that joy

20   could not show itself modest enough without a badge of
bitterness.

LEONATO Did he break out into tears?

MESSENGER In great measure.

I. i （第一幕第一场，后类推）（以下黑体数字为行码）

1 **Don** [dɔn]：唐，西班牙语的"先生"。　**Arragon**：阿拉贡，西班牙北部地区名，唐·彼德罗的封地。西班牙的阿拉贡亲王唐·彼德罗在平定私生子兄弟唐·约翰参加的叛乱后，来到老友兼属下梅西那总督里奥那托家做客。

2 **Messina** [me'si:nə]：梅西那，西西里岛北端城市。

3 **by this**：by this time.

4 **leagues** [li:g]：里格（长度名，约为三英里）。

6 **action**：battle.

7 **But few of any sort**：only a few ordinary men.　**of name**：of reputation；of noble family.

8 **twice itself**：doubled.

9 **full numbers**：全部人马。

11—12 **Much deserved on his part**：well deserved by him.　**equally remembered**：justly rewarded.　**hath borne himself**：has carried (or acquitted, behaved) himself，表现得…；行动得…。　**hath**：has 在中世纪和诗体英语中，第三人称单数动词用(e) th 结尾。

12—13 **beyond the promise of his age**：beyond what is to be expected of so young a man as he.

13—14 **figure of a lamb … feats of a lion**：既对称，又含双声头韵。

14—15 **feats** [fi:ts]：武艺；武功。　**hath … better bettered expectation**：has gone beyond people's expectations；has done more than is expected of him，超过人们对他的期望。　**better bettered**：better improved，这里使用词的重复，作文字游戏。

16—17 **will**：之前省略关系代词 who，在莎剧中关系代词作主语时被省略是常见的。　**very much glad**：very glad.

19—21 **joy could not show itself modest enough**：莎剧中常将抽象名词拟人化，但人称代词常用 it，这里是一个例子。拟人化(personification)使抽象名词大大地增添了形象性和感染力。　**modest**：moderate.　**badge**：仆人胸前佩戴的刻有主人家徽的金属牌。　**joy … bitterness**：欢乐达到如此的强度，如果不流下一些眼泪表明自己是忧愁的仆人，那就会显得他自己(指欢乐)不够谦虚了。

20—21 **badge of bitterness**：sign that joy is servant to sorrow，表示欢乐是忧愁的仆人的一种标志，在这里意指流泪。

22 **break out into tears**：现在习用 burst into tears，或 break out in tears.

LEONATO A kind overflow of kindness. There are no
25   faces truer than those that are so washed. How much
better is it to weep at joy than to joy at weeping!

BEATRICE I pray you, is Signior Mountanto returned
from the wars or no?

MESSENGER I know none of that name, lady. There was
30   none such in the army of any sort.

LEONATO What is he that you ask for, niece?

HERO My cousin means Signior Benedick of Padua.

MESSENGER O, he's returned, and as pleasant as ever he
was.

BEATRICE He set up his bills here in Messina and chal-
35   lenged Cupid at the flight, and my uncle's fool reading
the challenge, subscribed for Cupid and challenged him
at the burbolt. I pray you, how many hath he killed and
eaten in these wars? But how many hath he killed? For
indeed I promised to eat all of his killing.

40   LEONATO Faith, niece, you tax Signior Benedick too
much; but he'll be meet with you, I doubt it not.

MESSENGER He hath done good service, lady, in these wars.

BEATRICE You had musty victual, and he hath holp to
eat it. He is a very valiant trencherman; he hath an ex-
45   cellent stomach.

MESSENGER And a good soldier too, lady.

BEATRICE And a good soldier to a lady; but what is he to
a lord?

MESSENGER A lord to a lord, a man to a man; stuffed
50   with all honorable virtues.

BEATRICE It is so indeed. He is no less than a stuffed
man; but for the stuffing—well, we are all mortal.

LEONATO You must not, sir, mistake my niece. There is
a kind of merry war betwixt Signior Benedick and her.
55   They never meet but there's a skirmish of wit between
them.

24—25 **kind**：natural. **kindness**：tenderness. **A kind overflow of kindness**：这里 kind 一词二意，为双关语（pun），在莎剧中双关语使用得很多。 **There … washed**：这是一个表强调的句型，用否定词加比较级来强调说明被比较的事物达到最高的程度，等于说 The faces that are so washed（i. e. by tears）are the truest faces.

25—26 **How … weeping!**：这句话结合了重复（repetition）、对照（antithesis）及矛盾语（oxymoron）三种修辞手段，生动有力。

27 **Signior** [ˈsiːnjɔː]（意大利语）：先生（现在拼法为 Signor）. **Mountanto**（montanto）：比剑时向上挑刺的动作。 **Signior Mountanto**：劈刺先生。这是贝特丽丝给培尼狄克取的绰号，讥笑他好和人斗口。 **is … returned**：has returned. 伊丽莎白时代像 return 这类 verbs of motion 可以这样用。

30 **none such**：no such man；not such a man. **sort**：rank.

31 **he**：the man. **ask for**：ask about.

33 **pleasant**：merry；given to joking. 爱说笑的；爱打趣的。

34 **set up his bills**：posted notices，张贴启事（即下文说的 challenge）. 此段系用过去时，指前一次他来梅西那时所做的事。

35 **Cupid** [ˈkjuːpid]：希腊神话中的小爱神丘比特，为手持弓箭的眼瞎裸体的男孩，他的箭射中谁，谁就陷入情网。 **flight**：long-range archery，远距离射箭比赛（意思是培尼狄克自吹为 a better lady-killer, a "tyrant to their sex"）. **my uncle's fool**：旧时国王、贵族常雇来弄臣小丑，供逗乐解闷。里奥那托是公爵，也有一个 fool.

36 **subscribed for Cupid**：signed his name as Cupid's representative，在挑战书上代替丘比特签名应战。

37 **burbolt** [ˈbəːbɔːlt]：bird bolt，孩子射鸟玩的钝头小箭。贝特丽丝说培尼狄克这种箭，是取笑他的无能。 **how many**：how many birds.

38 **But how many**：but how many people.

40 **Faith**：in faith 或 by my faith 的简缩语，用作感叹词。 **tax**：disparage，accuse，指责，挖苦。

41 **meet**（adj.）：even；quits. 他会和你旗鼓相当。

43 **victual** [ˈvitl]：食物（这里指军粮）. **holp**：helped；help 的这种屈折式过去分词，在伊丽莎白时代仍沿用，以后被淘汰。

44 **trencherman**：trencher 为旧时盛食物的木盘或里面的食物，因此 trencherman 的意思为 eater（食者），尤指食量大的人。

47 **to**：in comparison to.

49—50 **lord**：贵族男子。 **man**：男子汉。 **stuffed with**：filled with；full of.

51—52 **stuffed man**：figure stuffed to look like a man；dummy，里面塞满了东西的假人；草包。

52 **but for**：except for. **but … mortal**：要不是靠里面塞的东西——唉，别说算了，我们都不过是凡人（意思是：我们也都是要吃饭的，也就是说都是肚子里要塞东西的）。

55 **skirmish of wit**：斗智，舌战。

BEATRICE   Alas, he gets nothing by that! In our last
conflict four of his five wits went halting off, and now
is the whole man governed with one; so that if he have
60   wit enough to keep himself warm, let him bear it for a
difference between himself and his horse; for it is all
the wealth that he hath left to be known a reasonable
creature. Who is his companion now? He hath every
month a new sworn brother.

65   MESSENGER   Is't possible?

BEATRICE   Very easily possible. He wears his faith but as
the fashion of his hat; it ever changes with the next block.

MESSENGER   I see, lady, the gentleman is not in your books.

BEATRICE   No. An he were, I would burn my study. But
70   I pray you, who is his companion? Is there no young
squarer now that will make a voyage with him to the
devil?

MESSENGER   He is most in the company of the right noble
Claudio.

75   BEATRICE   O Lord, he will hang upon him like a disease!
He is sooner caught than the pestilence, and the taker
runs presently mad. God help the noble Claudio! If he
have caught the Benedick, it will cost him a thousand
pound ere 'a be cured.

80   MESSENGER   I will hold friends with you, lady.

BEATRICE   Do, good friend.

LEONATO   You will never run mad, niece.

BEATRICE   No, not till a hot January.

MESSENGER   Don Pedro is approached.

*Enter Don Pedro, Claudio, Benedick, Balthasar, and
John the Bastard.*

85   PEDRO   Good Signior Leonato, are you come to meet your
trouble? The fashion of the world is to avoid cost, and
you encounter it.

58   five wits：中世纪英国俗称人有五种智能，即常识（common sense）、想象（imagination）、幻想（fantasy）、判断（estimation）和记忆（memory），近似汉语"六神无主"这一短语中的"六神"。   **halting**：limping 指舌战之后，培尼狄克的五种智能中有四种被打得一瘸一拐地逃走了。

59   if he have：伊丽莎白时代用动词原形表达虚拟语气现在时。

60—61   keep himself warm：使自己不成为冷血动物。   **bear it for a difference**（纹章用语）：贵族的小房或年轻成员佩戴该族的纹章时，采用一种区别的标记。此句说他和马已经差不多。

62—63   to be known（as）**a reasonable creature**：被称为有理性的动物（即人）。

64   sworn brother：结义弟兄。

66—67   faith：loyalty to one's oath，对誓言的恪守。   **but as**：only as.   **He … hat**：他对结义时的誓言三心二意（即经常换朋友），就像他经常换帽子式样一般。   **block**：hat-block；mould. 帽子的模子。

68   not in your（good）**books**：not in your favour；not on the list of your friends.

69   An：if.   **my study**：all my books.

71   squarer：a boisterous quarrelsome fellow.

73   right（adj.）：rightful；veritable.

76—77   caught：contracted，传染上。   **pestilence**：瘟疫主要指鼠疫，是 16 世纪英国伦敦常发生的传染病。   **taker**：传染上的人。**runs presently mad**：immediately goes mad.

78—79   a thousand pound：a thousand pounds（pound 为单数指复数，这是当时的一种用法）。   **ere**：before.   **'a**：是古体 ha，he 的口语省读形式。   **ere 'a be cured**：before he is cured.

80   hold friends with you：be careful to remain friendly with you.（言外之意是：如果得罪了你，你的挖苦话可令人难以招架呀！）

81   Do：Do hold friends with me.

82   You … mad：你绝不会发疯的（也就是说"你绝不会染上 Benedick 瘟病的"）。

83   hot January：酷热的一月（这是不可能出现的事）。

85—86   meet your trouble：迎接你的麻烦事（指招待一个贵族客人的麻烦）。

87   encounter：go to meet.

LEONATO   Never came trouble to my house in the likeness
of your grace; for trouble being gone, comfort should
90   remain; but when you depart from me, sorrow abides
and happiness takes his leave.

PEDRO   You embrace your charge too willingly. I think
this is your daughter.

LEONATO   Her mother hath many times told me so.

95   BENEDICK   Were you in doubt, sir, that you asked her?

LEONATO   Signior Benedick, no; for then were you a child.

PEDRO   You have it full, Benedick. We may guess by this
what you are, being a man. Truly the lady fathers
herself. Be happy, lady, for you are like an honorable
100   father.

BENEDICK   If Signior Leonato be her father, she would
not have his head on her shoulders for all Messina, as
like him as she is.

BEATRICE   I wonder that you will still be talking, Signior
105   Benedick. Nobody marks you.

BENEDICK   What, my dear Lady Disdain! Are you yet living?

BEATRICE   Is it possible Disdain should die while she hath
such meet food to feed it as Signior Benedick? Courtesy
110   itself must convert to Disdain if you come in her presence.

BENEDICK   Then is courtesy a turncoat. But it is certain I
am loved of all ladies, only you excepted; and I would I
could find in my heart that I had not a hard heart, for
truly I love none.

115   BEATRICE   A dear happiness to women! They would else
have been troubled with a pernicious suitor. I thank
God and my cold blood, I am of your humor for that. I
had rather hear my dog bark at a crow than a man
swear he loves me.

120   BENEDICK   God keep your ladyship still in that mind! So

88—91 Never came trouble …：never would trouble come ….
Never … leave：在里奥那托的这段话中，trouble、comfort、sorrow 和 happiness 这些抽象名词都被拟人化了，仿佛它们是可以来做客或与主人告别的人似的。

89 your grace：殿下（对彼德罗亲王的尊称）。

92 embrace：welcome or receive something joyfully. **charge**：expense and responsibility. 本剧描写当时宫廷贵族讲俏皮话成风，连里奥那托总督也是这样。

95 that：so that.

96 for … child：意思是：当时你还小，不可能勾引我的妻子。

97 You have it full：You are fully answered，这句答话够你受的了。 **by this**：by this remark，从这句话。

98—99 being a man：既然你现在长大成人了。 **fathers herself**：resembles and so indicates her father，极像她父亲，这点正说明她确实是她父亲的女儿。

101—102 would … shoulders：有两义：一、不愿他那满是白发和胡须的头长在她自己的肩上。二、不愿有他那些庸俗的思想。培尼狄克用这句话回报里奥那托对他的挖苦。

102—103 for all Messina：even with the entire city of Messina as a reward，即令把整个梅西那城都送给她，她也不会愿意换上她父亲的脑袋。 **as like him as she is**：however much she may be like him.

104 will still be talking：will 要重读，表示坚持做某事，进行时是指持续做某事。 **still**：always.

105 marks：notices.

106 Lady Disdain：傲慢小姐（培尼狄克给贝特丽丝起的绰号）。

108 Disdain should die：Disdain 拟人化了，所以大写，其后的人称代词既用 she，接着又用 it，莎士比亚是灵活使用的。下文 Courtesy 的人称代词也是如此。

109 meet：suitable.

110 convert（v. i.）：change.

111 turncoat：person who changes sides，变节者。

112 of：by. **only you excepted**：only you being an exception，只有你是例外（为独立主格结构，excepted 为过去分词）。

115 dear happiness：great fortune. **else**（adv.）：otherwise.

116 pernicious：mischievous；malicious；wicked.

117 of your humor for that：of your frame（or state）of mind on that point.

120 mind：frame of mind. **So**：so that.

some gentleman or other shall 'scape a predestinate
scratched face.

BEATRICE Scratching could not make it worse an 'twere
such a face as yours were.

125 BENEDICK Well, you are a rare parrot-teacher.

BEATRICE A bird of my tongue is better than a beast of
yours.

BENEDICK I would my horse had the speed of your
tongue, and so good a continuer. But keep your way,

130 i' God's name! I have done.

BEATRICE You always end with a jade's trick. I know
you of old.

PEDRO That is the sum of all, Leonato. Signior Claudio
and Signior Benedick, my dear friend Leonato hath in-

135 vited you all. I tell him we shall stay here at the least a
month, and he heartily prays some occasion may detain
us longer. I dare swear he is no hypocrite, but prays
from his heart.

LEONATO If you swear, my lord, you shall not be for-

140 sworn. [*to Don John*] Let me bid you welcome, my
lord. Being reconciled to the Prince your brother, I owe
you all duty.

JOHN I thank you. I am not of many words, but I thank
you.

145 LEONATO Please it your grace lead on?

PEDRO Your hand, Leonato. We will go together.

Exeunt. Manent Benedick and Claudio.

CLAUDIO Benedick, didst thou note the daughter of Signior Leonato?

150 BENEDICK I noted her not, but I looked on her.

CLAUDIO Is she not a modest young lady?

BENEDICK Do you question me as an honest man should
do, for my simple true judgment? or would you have
me speak after my custom, as being a professed tyrant

121 shall：will 伊丽莎白时代 shall 常有和现在 will 一样的意思和用法。　**'scape**：escape.　**predestinate** [pri'destinit]：predestinated 末尾的 d 由于在 t 音之后因省略而脱落。

123 an 'twere：if it were.

124 as yours were：as your face is（因 if 从句中的动词 were 系虚拟语气，表示与事实不符的假设，这里跟着用了 were）。

125 rare parrot-teacher：fine chatterer, who repeats himself.

126—127 a beast of yours：a beast of your tongue, i. e. , a dumb beast.

129 continuer：one having the power to keep going.　**keep your way**：只管说下去吧。

130 done：finished.

131 jade's trick：劣马的诡计，指突然停住，退出比赛。

133 That … all：That's all，就这样讲定了。

135 at the least：at least.

136 occasion：cause，原因。

139—140 be forsworn：break your oath，违背誓言。

141 Being reconciled to the Prince：since you are reconciled to Don Pedro（Don John 叛乱被打败，假意悔罪，和 Don Pedro 言归于好）。

145 Please … on?：Will your grace please lead on?

146 Your hand：Let me take your hand.

147 *Exeunt* [拉丁语,'eksiʌnt]：go out（第三人称复数现在式，为 exit 的复数）。

148 thou：第二人称单数代词主格。这里克劳狄奥对熟人培尼狄克称 thou，是友爱的表示，足见他认真地想征求培尼狄克的意见。反之，培尼狄克仍用一般的 you，并多开玩笑。莎剧中用 you 还是用 thou 很有讲究，值得注意。接 thou 的动词多用(e)st 结尾。thou 的宾格是 thee，所有格是 thy, thine.　**note**：notice especially.

150 I noted her not, but I looked on her：我看见她了，但没有对她特别注意。

153 for：to seek.

154 after my custom：according to my habit.　**professed**：公开宣称的。

155   to their sex?

CLAUDIO No, I pray thee speak in sober judgment.

BENEDICK Why, i' faith, methinks she's too low for a high praise, too brown for a fair praise, and too little for a great praise. Only this commendation I can afford

160   her, that were she other than she is, she were unhandsome, and being no other but as she is, I do not like her.

CLAUDIO Thou thinkest I am in sport. I pray thee tell me truly how thou lik'st her.

165 BENEDICK Would you buy her, that you enquire after her?

CLAUDIO Can the world buy such a jewel?

BENEDICK Yea, and a case to put it into. But speak you this with a sad brow? or do you play the flouting Jack,

170   to tell us Cupid is a good hare-finder and Vulcan a rare carpenter? Come, in what key shall a man take you to go in the song?

CLAUDIO In mine eye she is the sweetest lady that ever I looked on.

175 BENEDICK I can see yet without spectacles, and I see no such matter. There's her cousin, an she were not possessed with a fury, exceeds her as much in beauty as the first of May doth the last of December. But I hope you have no intent to turn husband, have

180   you?

CLAUDIO I would scarce trust myself, though I had sworn the contrary, if Hero would be my wife.

BENEDICK Is't come to this? In faith, hath not the world one man but he will wear his cap with sus-

185   picion? Shall I never see a bachelor of threescore again? Go to, i' faith! An thou wilt needs thrust thy neck into a yoke, wear the print of it and sigh away Sundays. Look! Don Pedro is returned to seek

157—158　i' faith：indeed；truly。　**methinks**：I think。　**she's too low for a high praise**：故意用 low，不用 short，以与 high 相对。

158　fair praise：fair 作 favorable 解，同时指皮肤白，与 brown 相对。　**little**：个子小（与 great 相对）。

160—161　were … unhandsome：if she were different from what she is，she would be ugly。　**but**：than。

163　in sport：in play，开玩笑。　**I … me**：I beg you to tell me。

165　enquire after：enquire about。

167　Can the world buy such a jewel?：能用全世界买这样一颗珍珠么？

168　Yea：Yes。

169　sad brow：serious countenance，一本正经的面孔。　**flouting Jack**：mocking knave，嘲弄者。

170　hare-finder：猎野兔的能手。　**Vulcan** [ˈvʌlkən]：希腊神话中的锻冶神。Cupid 眼瞎不能猎兔，Vulcan 系铁匠不是木匠，因此这些都是胡说。

171—172　in what key shall a man take you to go（join）**in the song?**：人家要知道你唱的是什么调，才能与你相和。

177　possessed with：dominated by。　**fury**：希腊神话中生有蛇发的复仇女神。　**possessed with a fury**：为复仇女神所缠住，意为像凶神恶煞似地性情泼辣。　**exceeds**：前面省略 who。

181—182　scarce：scarcely。　**had sworn the contrary**：发了反面的誓（即发誓不结婚）。

182　would be：should be willing to be。

183—185　hath not the world one man but he will wear his cap with suspicion?：难道世界上没有一个男人不愿意被人怀疑戴上了绿帽子么？（not … but … 为一句型，等于 not … that not … 没有…不…） **wear his cap with suspicion**：be suspected of wearing a cap to hide his cuckold's horns，被人怀疑戴帽子是为了要掩盖他当了王八后头上长出的两只角（西方有妻子不贞时，丈夫头上长角这一说法）。　**three-score**：sixty。

186　Go to（仅用于祈使语气）：exclamation of impatience，incredulity，etc.（表示不耐烦、不相信等的感叹语）得了吧！去你的吧！ **wilt needs**：must。

187—188　yoke：牛轭（这里指婚姻的枷锁）。　**wear the print of it**：永远带上它（牛轭）压在颈上的印痕。　**sigh away Sundays**：用叹息消磨掉一个又一个星期天（指星期天休息，只好在家与妻子相对而坐，百无聊赖）。

you.

190   *Enter Don Pedro.*

PEDRO   What secret hath held you here, that you fol-
lowed not to Leonato's?

BENEDICK   I would your grace would constrain me to
tell.

195   PEDRO   I charge thee on thy allegiance.

BENEDICK   You hear, Count Claudio. I can be secret as
a dumb man, I would have you think so; but, on
my allegiance — mark you this — on my allegiance!
he is in love. With who? Now that is your grace's

200   part. Mark how short his answer is: With Hero, Leonato's short daughter.

CLAUDIO   If this were so, so were it uttered.

BENEDICK   Like the old tale, my lord: 'It is not so, nor
'twas not so; but indeed, God forbid it should be so!'

205   CLAUDIO   If my passion change not shortly, God forbid it
should be otherwise.

PEDRO   Amen, if you love her, for the lady is very well
worthy.

CLAUDIO   You speak this to fetch me in, my lord.

210   PEDRO   By my troth, I speak my thought.

CLAUDIO   And, in faith, my lord, I spoke mine.

BENEDICK   And, by my two faiths and troths, my lord, I
spoke mine.

CLAUDIO   That I love her, I feel.

215   PEDRO   That she is worthy, I know.

BENEDICK   That I neither feel how she should be loved,
nor know how she should be worthy, is the opinion
that fire cannot melt out of me. I will die in it at the
stake.

220   PEDRO   Thou wast ever an obstinate heretic in the despite
of beauty.

CLAUDIO   And never could maintain his part but in the

193 **constrain**：force.

195 **on thy allegiance**：with your loyalty tó me, your prince, as guarantee.

197—198 **but, on my allegiance**：但现在要凭我对君王的忠诚说话（即我不能不说，如果不说就对你不忠）。这一段话，but 以前对 Claudio 说，but 以后对 Don Pedro 说。

199—200 **With who?**：With whom? **that is your grace's part** (to ask that question)：那是殿下问的话。 **part**：（舞台用语）台词。 **short**：（双关语）既指回答简短，又指 Hero 身材矮小。

202 **If this were so, so were it uttered**：If I had told him such a secret, he would have revealed it in this way. (Claudio 在 Don Pedro 面前故意闪烁其词。)

203 **old tale**：可能指兰胡子的故事，其中恶人一再否认自己的罪行，并说"It is not so, nor 'twas not so, but, indeed, God forbid it should be so!"（现在不是这么一回事，过去也不是，愿上帝禁止发生这样的事。）最后面对物证，他不得不认罪。

205—206 **God forbid it should be otherwise**：Claudio 的否认也是欲盖弥彰。

207 **Amen** [希伯来语，ɑːˈmen]：Certainly; So be it (基督教祈祷结尾时的祝愿和附和词)。

209 **fetch me in**：get me to confess.

210 **troth**：truth; true word. **By my troth**：我发誓。

212 **by my two faiths and troths**：凭我分别对你们两位的忠心（暗指我的忠心具有两面性）。

214 **That I love her, I feel**：这句把宾语从句放在句首，表示强调。以下两人的话也类似。

218—219 **I will die in it at the stake**：这里 it 指 opinion, at the stake (在火刑柱上)指中世纪天主教会对异教徒残酷迫害的一种方法：我宁可烧死在火刑柱上也不会改变这个看法。

220 **despite**：spiting, 轻蔑。

222—223 **never could maintain his part but in the force of his will**：要不是顽固地不认输（毫无道理地坚持己见），他这个角色也不可能继续扮演下去。

force of his will.

BENEDICK That a woman conceived me, I thank her; that
225   she brought me up, I likewise give her most humble
thanks; but that I will have a rechate winded in my
forehead, or hang my bugle in an invisible baldrick,
all women shall pardon me. Because I will not do them
the wrong to mistrust any, I will do myself the right to
230   trust none; and the fine is (for the which I may go the
finer), I will live a bachelor.

PEDRO I shall see thee, ere I die, look pale with love.

BENEDICK With anger, with sickness, or with hunger,
my lord, not with love. Prove that ever I lose more
235   blood with love than I will get again with drinking,
pick out mine eyes with a ballad-maker's pen and hang
me up at the door of a brothel house for the sign of
blind Cupid.

PEDRO Well, if ever thou dost fall from this faith, thou
240   wilt prove a notable argument.

BENEDICK If I do, hang me in a bottle like a cat and shoot
at me; and he that hits me, let him be clapped on the
shoulder and called Adam.

PEDRO Well, as time shall try.

245   'In time the savage bull doth bear the yoke. '

BENEDICK The savage bull may, but if ever the sensible
Benedick bear it, pluck off the bull's horns and set
them in my forehead, and let me be vilely painted, and
in such great letters as they write 'Here is good horse
250   to hire,' let them signify under my sign 'Here you
may see Benedick the married man. '

CLAUDIO If this should ever happen, thou wouldst be
horn-mad.

PEDRO Nay, if Cupid have not spent all his quiver in
255   Venice, thou wilt quake for this shortly.

BENEDICK I look for an earthquake too, then.

224   conceived：怀孕。

226—227   rechate：召回猎狗的号角声。   **winded**（sounded）**in my forehead**：前额发出号角声。

227   baldrick：猎人斜佩在胸前用以悬挂号角的带子。明的或暗的角，均指妻子不贞时丈夫头上长角。暗指女人都要偷汉。

230—231   fine：finis；conclusion.   **the which**：which 原是非特定形容词，故旧时一种用法可在前面加 the.   **go the finer**：穿着得更漂亮（因为省下了供养妻子的费用）。

234—236   lose ··· drinking：过去认为每叹一口气就要耗掉一滴血，而酒却能生血。   **Prove that ever I lose ···, pick out ···**：= If you can prove ···, you may pick out ···，如果你能证明···，那就请挖掉···。

236   pick ··· pen：用歌谣作者的笔挖掉我的眼珠（旧时流行一种新闻歌谣，多涉及时事及社会丑闻，印在单页上，供朗诵、歌唱或出售）。

237—238   for：as.   **sign of blind Cupid**：the usual sign hung before a brothel，当时英国妓院门口的招牌上，常画着蒙着眼睛的小爱神丘比特。

239   fall from this faith：depart from this belief.

240   notable：remarkable，显著的，臭名昭著的（常用于贬义）。 **argument**：subject；topic for conversation.

241   bottle：wicker basket，cage，柳条笼子。   **hang me in a bottle like a cat**：过去有时把活猫关在柳条笼子中作为箭靶。

243   Adam：Adam Bell 歌谣中所歌颂的一个神箭手，见 Percy's Reliques.

244   try：prove.

245   'In ··· yoke'：不准确地引自 Thomas Kyd's "*The Spanish Tragedy*"（about 1592）II. i 3 行"In time the savage bull sustains the yoke." Kyd 又引自 Thomas Watson's *Hecatompathia*（1582），sonnet 47. 希腊、罗马神话中天神垂爱女郎 Europa，化为公牛，将她驮走。

246   sensible：rational.

250   signify：indicate.

253   horn-mad：双关语 1. raving mad，狂怒的（公牛怒时以角撞人）；2. mad with jealousy，丈夫妒火中烧（男子因妻子失贞，头上长角）。

254—255   in Venice：旧时威尼斯城以妓女众多出名。quiver，quake，earthquake 这三个词均含 qu 音，意义上也有联系，构成文字游戏。quiver 为双关语，表"箭囊"，又可表"战栗"。quake 也表"战栗"。

256   I look for an earthquake too, then：如果说我会发抖，那除非是发生了地震，使我身不由己地抖起来。

PEDRO   Well, you will temporize with the hours. In
the meantime, good Signior Benedick, repair   to
Leonato's, commend me to him and tell him I will not
260   fail him at supper; for indeed he hath made great preparation.

BENEDICK   I have almost matter enough in me for such an
embassage, and so I commit you —

CLAUDIO   To the tuition of God. From my house — if I
265   had it —

PEDRO   The sixth of July. Your loving friend, Benedick.

BENEDICK   Nay, mock not, mock not. The body of your
discourse is sometime guarded with fragments, and the
270   guards are but slightly basted on neither. Ere you flout
old ends any further, examine your conscience. And so
I leave you.   *Exit.*

CLAUDIO

My liege, your highness now may do me good.

PEDRO

My love is thine to teach. Teach it but how,
275   And thou shalt see how apt it is to learn
Any hard lesson that may do thee good.

CLAUDIO

Hath Leonato any son, my lord?

PEDRO

No child but Hero; she's his only heir.
Dost thou affect her, Claudio?

CLAUDIO   O my lord,
280   When you went onward on this ended action,
I looked upon her with a soldier's eye,
That liked, but had a rougher task in hand
Than to drive liking to the name of love;
But now I am returned and that war-thoughts
285   Have left their places vacant, in their rooms

257 temporize：comply；weaken one's position.   **with the hours**：hour by hour.

258 repair：go.

262 matter：sense.

263 embassage：mission.

264—265 To the tuition of God：Claudio 不等 Benedick 说完，补足了他的话，成为信末套语，意为"愿上帝保佑你"。   **tuition**：care；protection.   **From my house — if I had it —**：自家中发，如果我有一个家的话。

269 sometime：sometimes.   **guarded**：①trimmed，镶了…边，用…装饰；②protected，用…防护。

270—271 guards：①装饰性镶边；②防护物。   **slightly basted on**：slightly sewn on；roughly stitched on（on 为副词），稍为缝上的；缝得不牢的。   **neither (adv.)**：for all that；nevertheless（用于否定词 no, not, nor 等后或 but（＝only；merely 仅仅）后表示强调。现已不这样用，而改用 either）.   **flout old ends**：mock with old fragments，用陈旧的不成句的言语来开玩笑。

273 My liege, your highness：君主、殿下都是对 Don Pedro 的尊称。从这一行起到本场末，从散文改用素体韵文，即抑扬格五音步（十音节）诗行，表示比较文雅的谈吐。

274 My love is thine to teach：My love is yours，please teach me how I may serve you. 我极愿为你效劳。

275 apt：willing，ready，乐意。

277 Hath Leonato any son, my lord?：Claudio 的这句问话，表明他对婚姻的谨慎态度，目的在了解 Hero 的经济继承状况，可见他是一个很讲究实际的青年。

279 affect：care for.

280 ended action：war that is now over.

283 drive liking to the name of love：把（对她的）喜爱增进为爱情。

284 now I：now that I.

285 in their rooms：in their room（room 作空间、余地解时，现为不可数名词，旧时可用复数）。

Come thronging soft and delicate desires,
All prompting me how fair young Hero is,
Saying I liked her ere I went to wars.

PEDRO

Thou wilt be like a lover presently

290   And tire the hearer with a book of words.
If thou dost love fair Hero, cherish it,
And I will break with her and with her father,
And thou shalt have her. Was't not to this end
That thou began'st to twist so fine a story?

CLAUDIO

295   How sweetly you do minister to love,
That know love's grief by his complexion!
But lest my liking might too sudden seem,
I would have salved it with a longer treatise.

PEDRO

What need the bridge much broader than the flood?

300   The fairest grant is the necessity.
Look, what will serve is fit. 'Tis once, thou lovest,
And I will fit thee with the remedy.
I know we shall have revelling to-night.
I will assume thy part in some disguise

305   And tell fair Hero I am Claudio,
And in her bosom I'll unclasp my heart
And take her hearing prisoner with the force
And strong encounter of my amorous tale.
Then after to her father will I break,

310   And the conclusion is, she shall be thine.
In practice let us put it presently.   *Exeunt.*

287 **prompting**：reminding.

288 **Saying**：逻辑主语是 soft and delicate desires.

292 **break with her**：broach the matter with her，向她透露此事。

294 **twist so fine a story**?：三弯九曲地说出这件美事。

295 **minister to**：give help or service to.

296 **That know**：who know（关系代词 that 过去可用于非限制性
定语从句中，现在用 who）.   **his complexion!**：love's（the lover's）ap-
pearance（paleness），情人苍白的脸色。

298 **salved**：accounted for.   **treatise**：discourse；speech.

300 **The … necessity**：The best gift is what satisfies the need.

301 **what**：whatever.   **'Tis once**：briefly；in a word.

302 **fit**：supply.

303 **revelling**（n.）：宴乐。

306 **in her bosom**：privately to her.   **unclasp**：旧时书册用金属钩
子 clasps 扣紧，unclasp 是开卷，倾吐。

307 **take her hearing prisoner**：capture her hearing.

308 **encounter**：meeting；combat，遭 遇；交 锋。take prisoner，
force，encounter 都是借用军事用语。

311 **In … presently**：Let us put it in practice at once.

SCENE II

A room in Leonato's house

Enter Leonato and an old man [Antonio],
brother to Leonato [meeting].

LEONATO How now, brother? Where is my cousin your
son? Hath he provided this music?

ANTONIO He is very busy about it. But, brother, I can
tell you strange news that you yet dreamt not of.

5 LEONATO Are they good?

ANTONIO As the event stamps them; but they have a
good cover, they show well outward. The Prince and
Count Claudio, walking in a thick-pleached alley in
mine orchard, were thus much overheard by a man of

10 mine: the Prince discovered to Claudio that he loved
my niece your daughter and meant to acknowledge it
this night in a dance, and if he found her accordant, he
meant to take the present time by the top and instantly
break with you of it.

15 LEONATO Hath the fellow any wit that told you this?

ANTONIO A good sharp fellow. I will send for him, and
question him yourself.

LEONATO No, no. We will hold it as a dream till it
appear itself; but I will acquaint my daughter withal,

20 that she may be the better prepared for an answer, if
peradventure this be true. Go you and tell her of it.

Exit Antonio.

Enter Antonio's son with a Musician.

Cousin, you know what you have to do. — [*to the*
25 *Musician*] O, I cry you mercy, friend. Go you with
me, and I will use your skill. — Good cousin, have a
care this busy time.   *Exeunt.*

I. ii

  1 **cousin**: used loosely for any kinsman, here a nephew.

  2 **Hath he provided this music?**: Has he arranged for the music? Has he got together the musicians? (i. e., for the ball to be held in honor of the distinguished guests.)

  4 **that you yet dreamt not of**: which you did not dream of.

  5 **they**: news (Shakespeare used "news" in both the singular and plural numbers).

  6 **event**: outcome.   **stamps**: impresses; prints.   **them**: the news, the book of news. 此句指 It depends upon how things turn out.

  7 **cover**: 封面。转义 outward appearance.

  8 **thick-pleached alley**: garden walk sheltered by thickly interwoven boughs.

  9 **mine orchard**: "mine" was sometimes used before a vowel. **orchard**: garden.   **man**: servant.

  10 **discovered**: revealed.

  12 **accordant**: agreeable.

  13—14 **take … top**: take time by the forelock, seize the moment. **top**: forelock, 马额毛。   **break with you of it**: disclose it to you.

  15 **wit**: intelligence, good sense.   **that**: who.

  16 **sharp**: acute; shrewd.

  18 **hold**: regard.

  19—20 **appear**: the subjunctive present.   **withal**: with it. **that**: so that.

  21 **peradventure**: perhaps, by chance.

  25 **cry you mercy**: beg your pardon.

  26—27 **have a care**: please attend to things.

SCENE III

In front of Leonato's house

Enter Sir John the Bastard and Conrade, his companion.

CONRADE   What the goodyear, my lord! Why are you
thus out of measure sad?

JOHN   There is no measure in the occasion that breeds;
therefore the sadness is without limit.

5   CONRADE   You should hear reason.

JOHN   And when I have heard it, what blessing brings
it?

CONRADE   If not a present remedy, at least a patient sufferance.

10   JOHN   I wonder that thou (being, as thou say'st thou
art, born under Saturn) goest about to apply a moral
medicine to a mortifying mischief. I cannot hide what I
am: I must be sad when I have cause, and smile at no
man's jests; eat when I have stomach, and wait for no

15   man's leisure; sleep when I am drowsy, and tend on
no man's business; laugh when I am merry, and claw
no man in his humor.

CONRADE   Yea, but you must not make the full show of
this till you may do it without controlment. You have

20   of late stood out against your brother, and he hath
ta'en you newly into his grace, where it is impossible
you should take true root but by the fair weather that
you make yourself. It is needful that you frame the season for your own harvest.

25   JOHN   I had rather be a canker in a hedge than a rose
in his grace, and it better fits my blood to be dis-
dained of all than to fashion a carriage to rob love
from any. In this, though I cannot be said to be a
flattering honest man, it must not be denied but I am

I. iii

1   What the goodyear: what the deuce, used as a mild curse(温和的咒骂语)。

2   out of measure: excessively, 过分。

3   occasion: cause; reason; here it refers to the fact of his being a bastard.   **breeds**: causes it; gives rise to the sadness. 此句意为 The cause of my discontent is immeasurable.

5   hear: listen to, heed.

8—9   sufferance: endurance.

11   Saturn ['sætən]: 土星。据旧时西方占星术,生在土星上的人性情忧郁、阴沉。

12—13   mortifying mischief: fatal disease 指忧郁症 melancholy. 这里四个字都用 m 的头韵。全句意思是"I am surprised that you, who have almost as melancholic a nature as my own, should attempt to moralize to me about the incurable melancholy I am suffering from."   **what I am**: i. e., a royal bastard, 王室的私生子。

14   stomach: appetite.

15   tend on: attend to, 照料。

16—17   claw: scratch; flatter.   **in his humor**: according to his mood.

19   controlment: restraint. 此句意思是"只有将来你得意了,方能无所顾忌。"

20—21   stood out against: opposed, rebelled against.   **hath ta'en you newly into his grace**: has taken you into his favor only recently.   **where**: whereas.

**21—24   这段大意是:你只有设法创造适当的气候才能扎根,结果,得到收获。只有赢得彼得罗亲王的信任,才能实现自己的野心。

22   take true root: 扎根。

23   needful: necessary.   **frame**: contrive; bring to pass.

25   canker: dog-rose, 野蔷薇(一种荆棘)。

26—27   blood: ①disposition; ②status as a bastard of the royal blood.   **of**: by.

27   fashion a carriage: assume a manner, 装出样子。   **rob love**: gain undeserved affection, 窃取别人的好意。

29   flattering: pleasing.   **but**: 一般等于 that not, 但在这里等于 that. 在伊丽莎白时代, 有时 not … but 反反不得正, 这类双重否定的用法比较普遍。

30   a plain-dealing villain. I am trusted with a muzzle
        and enfranchised with a clog; therefore I have decre-
        ed not to sing in my cage. If I had my mouth, I
        would bite; if I had my liberty, I would do my liking.
        In the meantime let me be that I am, and seek not to
35   alter me.

   CONRADE Can you make no use of your discontent?

   JOHN I make all use of it, for I use it only. Who comes
        here? What news, Borachio?

            Enter Borachio.

40   BORACHIO I came yonder from a great supper. The
        Prince your brother is royally entertained by Leo-
        nato, and I can give you intelligence of an intended
        marriage.

   JOHN Will it serve for any model to build mischief on?
45   What is he for a fool that betroths himself to unquiet-
        ness?

   BORACHIO Marry, it is your brother's right hand.

   JOHN Who? the most exquisite Claudio?

   BORACHIO Even he.

50   JOHN A proper squire! And who? and who? which way
        looks he?

   BORACHIO Marry, one Hero, the daughter and heir of
        Leonato.

   JOHN A very forward March-chick! How came you to
55   this?

   BORACHIO Being entertained for a perfumer, as I was
        smoking a musty room, comes me the Prince and
        Claudio, hand in hand in sad conference. I whipt
        me behind the arras and there heard it agreed upon
60   that the Prince should woo Hero for himself, and hav-
        ing obtained her, give her to Count Claudio.

   JOHN Come, come, let us thither. This may prove food
        to my displeasure. That young start-up hath all the

30—31 muzzle：（动物的）口套，口络。 **enfranchised**：set free.
clog：（绑在动物腿上以阻碍行动的）重物，坠子。 **I … clog**：I am
trusted only when I am muzzled and allowed freedom only with a clog
tied to my leg，给我的信任和自由都是极有限的。

31—32 decreed：decided. **If I had my mouth**：If my mouth were
not muzzled.

34 that：what.

37 use it only：do nothing else but cultivate my discontent.

38 Borachio：源自西班牙语 borracha，装酒的革瓶，转义酒鬼。

40 yonder：over there 修饰 supper.

44 model：ground plan，design，设计图。

45—46 What is he for a fool：what kind of fool is he (for：as，be-
ing). **unquietness**：i. e.，a woman (implying that there is only noise
and bickering in a wife).

47 Marry：by the Virgin Mary，an exclamation meaning "indeed"，expressing surprise.

49 Even：used to emphasize the identity of a person.

50 proper squire：fine fellow(这里是反话)。

54—55 forward：precocious，早熟的。 **March-chick!**：三月孵出
的小鸡，早熟的雏儿。 **How came you to this?**：How did you come to
(or by) this information?

56 entertained for：employed as. **perfumer**：用燃香草的烟熏房
间的人。

57 comes me：这里的"me"是一种口头禅的语助词，有"for my
benefit"的意味。

58—59 sad：serious. **conference**：conversation. **whipt me**：
whipped me，moved quickly. (me 的用法同上) **arras**：挂毯(原产法国
东北部 Arras 镇)。

62—63 Come，come：(interjection expressing impatience)得啦，
得啦。 **let us thither**：let us go to that place or from here. **prove food
to**：feed，滋长。 **start-up**：upstart，骤贵者，暴发户。

glory of my overthrow. If I can cross him any way, I
65   bless myself every way. You are both sure, and will
assist me?

CONRADE To the death, my lord.

JOHN   Let us to the great supper. Their cheer is the
greater that I am subdued. Would the cook were o' my
70   mind! Shall we go prove what's to be done?

BORACHIO We'll wait upon your lordship.

Exit [*with others*].

64 **cross**：①thwart；②make the sign of the cross.

65 **bless**：benefit. **sure**：trustworthy.

67 **To the death**：till I die.

68 **Let us to**：Let us go to.

69—70 **that**：because. **Would**：I wish. **o' my mind!**：和我一样想法（能帮我毒死他们）。 **prove**：find out for ourselves. **go prove**：go and prove（Both in Shakespeare's time and now, the infinitive sign "to" may be omitted after "go", "come", etc).

71 **wait upon**：follow，accompany.

ACT II

SCENE I

The hall of Leonato's house

Enter Leonato, his brother [Antonio],
Hero his daughter, and Beatrice his
niece [also Margaret and Ursula].

LEONATO Was not Count John here at supper?

ANTONIO I saw him not.

BEATRICE How tartly that gentleman looks! I never can
see him but I am heart-burned an hour after.

5 HERO He is of a very melancholy disposition.

BEATRICE He were an excellent man that were made
just in the midway between him and Benedick. The
one is too like an image and says nothing, and the
other too like my lady's eldest son, evermore tattl-

10 ing.

LEONATO Then half Signior Benedick's tongue in Count
John's mouth, and half Count John's melancholy in
Signior Benedick's face —

BEATRICE With a good leg and a good foot, uncle,

15 and money enough in his purse, such a man would win
any woman in the world — if 'a could get her good
will.

LEONATO By my troth, niece, thou wilt never get thee a
husband if thou be so shrewd of thy tongue.

20 ANTONIO In faith, she's too curst.

BEATRICE Too curst is more than curst. I shall lessen
God's sending that way, for it is said, 'God sends a
curst cow short horns,' but to a cow too curst he sends

II. i

3 tartly：sourly.

4 after：afterwards.

6 He were：he would be.   **that were**：if he were.

7 in the midway between him and Benedick：正好是他和 Benedick 的折中。

8 image：statue.

9—10 my lady's eldest son：a noble lady's spoilt child. （英俗）长子有继承权,易受娇纵。   **evermore**：all the time.   **tattling**：prattling; talking.

14 a good leg and a good foot：匀称的腿、灵巧的脚,指身材好,又善跳舞。（这是用单数代替全体的用法）

16—17 'a：he.   **good will**：favor.

18 By my troth：by my faith, indeed （为加强语气用语）。   **get thee**：get for yourself.

19 shrewd：sharp.

20 curst：shrewish, malignant,说话尖刻。

21—22 第二个 curst：damned.   **that way**：in that respect.

22—23 'God sends a curst cow short horns'：（谚语）"上帝让脾气不好的牛只生短角",即没有伤人的力量。

none.

25 LEONATO So, by being too curst, God will send you no
horns.

BEATRICE Just, if he send me no husband; for the
which blessing I am at him upon my knees every
morning and evening. Lord, I could not endure a hus-
30 band with a beard on his face. I had rather lie in the
woollen!

LEONATO You may light on a husband that hath no
beard.

BEATRICE What should I do with him? dress him in
35 my apparel and make him my waiting gentlewoman?
He that hath a beard is more than a youth, and he
that hath no beard is less than a man; and he that
is more than a youth is not for me; and he that is
less than a man, I am not for him. Therefore I will
40 even take sixpence in earnest of the berrord and lead his
apes into hell.

LEONATO Well then, go you into hell?

BEATRICE No; but to the gate, and there will the devil
meet me like an old cuckold with horns on his head,
45 and say, 'Get you to heaven, Beatrice, get you to
heaven. Here's no place for you maids. ' So deliver I
up my apes, and away to Saint Peter. For the heavens;
he shows me where the bachelors sit, and there live we
as merry as the day is long.

50 ANTONIO [*to Hero*] Well, niece, I trust you will be ruled
by your father.

BEATRICE Yes, faith. It is my cousin's duty to make
cursy and say, 'Father, as it please you. ' But yet
for all that, cousin, let him be a handsome fellow,
55 or else make another cursy, and say, 'Father, as it
please me. '

LEONATO Well, niece, I hope to see you one day fitted

27—28 **Just**：just so.   **husband**：此处 Beatrice 玩文字游戏，因 horn 又可作男性生殖器解。   **for the which**：for which.

28 **at him**：insistently asking God.

30—31 **in the woollen!**：between rough blankets（instead of sheets）.

32 **light on**：find.

35 **waiting gentlewoman?**：贴身女仆。

40—41 **in earnest**：as deposit, as advance payment.   **of**：from. **berrord**：bear-ward，熊的看守者。当时纵犬斗熊是一种流行的马戏节目，管熊者也常兼管猴子。   **lead his apes into hell**：（英俗）老处女死后要到地狱去照管猴子，因为她们在世时，没有履行生儿育女的义务。

43 **but**：only.

44 **cuckold**：man whose wife is false to him.（英俗）丈夫头上长角，犹如我们说"戴绿头巾"。

47 **Saint Peter**：圣彼得（为掌管天国大门钥匙的人），见《圣经·新约·马太福音》第 16 章 19 节。

48 **bachelors**：unmarried men and women.

53 **cursy**：curtsy，妇女屈膝弯腰礼。   **please**：（虚拟语气）may please.

with a husband.

BEATRICE Not till God make men of some other metal
60   than earth. Would it not grieve a woman to be over-
mastered with a piece of valiant dust? to make an
account of her life to a clod of wayward marl? No,
uncle, I'll none. Adam's sons are my brethren, and
truly I hold it a sin to match in my kindred.

65   LEONATO Daughter, remember what I told you. If the
Prince do solicit you in that kind, you know your answer.

BEATRICE The fault will be in the music, cousin, if
you be not wooed in good time. If the Prince be
70   too important, tell him there is measure in everything, and so dance out the answer. For, hear me,
Hero: wooing, wedding, and repenting is as a
Scotch jig, a measure, and a cinquepace: the first
suit is hot and hasty like a Scotch jig (and full as
75   fantastical); the wedding, mannerly modest, as a
measure, full of state and ancientry; and then
comes Repentance and with his bad legs falls into
the cinquepace faster and faster, till he sink into his
grave.

80   LEONATO Cousin, you apprehend passing shrewdly.

BEATRICE I have a good eye, uncle; I can see a church by
daylight.

LEONATO The revellers are entering, brother. Make
good room.

85   *Enter* [*masked*] *Prince* [*Don*] *Pedro, Claudio,*
    and Benedick, and Balthasar; [*also, unmasked,*]
    Don John [*and Borachio, and musicians.*]

PEDRO Lady, will you walk about with your friend?

HERO So you walk softly and look sweetly and say noth-
90   ing, I am yours for the walk; and especially when I
walk away.

57—58 fitted with：matched with.

59 metal：①material；②mettle.

60 earth：根据《圣经·旧约·创世记》第 2 章，男人是上帝用土塑成的，而女人则是男人的肋骨变的。中世纪认为构成万物的四种元素：土、水、气、火，土最沉最纯。

61 with：by. **dust**：与 marl 同义。

62 clod of … marl?：piece of clay. **wayward**：任性的。

63 I'll none：I'll have none of them.

64 match in my kindred：marry a brother.

66 in that kind：in that way, i. e., concerning marriage.

69 time：双关语 1. measure；2. tempo in music.

70 important：importunate；pressing. **measure**：双关语 1. moderation；2. 跳舞节拍.

71 dance out the answer：利用跳舞拖延而不答。

73—74 Scotch jig：苏格兰快步舞。 **measure**：一种慢步而庄重的舞蹈。 **cinquepace**(法语 cinq pas)：five-step dance. **suit**：wooing.

75 fantastical：fanciful.

76 full（adv.）：fully. **state**：dignity. **ancientry**：old-fashioned formality.

77 Repentance：道德剧中"懊悔"一角，是瘸腿的老人。

78—79 sink … grave：死（cinque-pace 发音类似 sink apace，这里作谐音游戏）。

80 passing（adv.）：very.

83—84 Make good room：尽量让开些。

88 walk about：走一圈（在某些舞蹈中男女配对后绕场走一圈，作为开场）。 **friend**：partner.

89 So：so long as.

PEDRO   With me in your company?

HERO   I may say so when I please.

PEDRO   And when please you to say so?

HERO   When I like your favor, for God defend the lute
95   should be like the case!

PEDRO   My visor is Philemon's roof; within the house is
        Jove.

HERO   Why then, your visor should be thatched.

PEDRO   Speak low if you speak love.

100   *They step aside.*

BALTHASAR   Well, I would you did like me.

MARGARET   So would not I for your own sake, for I have
        many ill qualities.

BALTHASAR   Which is one?

110   MARGARET   I say my prayers aloud.

BALTHASAR   I love you the better. The hearers may cry
        amen.

MARGARET   God match me with a good dancer!

BALTHASAR   Amen.

115   MARGARET   And God keep him out of my sight when the
        dance is done! Answer, clerk.'

BALTHASAR   No more words. The clerk is answered.

            They step aside.

URSULA   I know you well enough. You are Signior
120   Antonio.

ANTONIO   At a word, I am not.

URSULA   I know you by the waggling of your head.

ANTONIO   To tell you true, I counterfeit him.

URSULA   You could never do him so ill-well unless you
125   were the very man. Here's his dry hand up and down.
        You are he, you are he!

ANTONIO   At a word, I am not.

URSULA   Come, come, do you think I do not know
        you by your excellent wit? Can virtue hide itself?

94 **favor**：face. **God defend**：God forbid. **lute**：像琵琶的一种拨弦琴。

95 **case**：琴盒。这里琴和琴盒比喻容貌和假面。Don Pedro 的假面很丑，故 Hero 说你的容貌可别像假面一样。

96 **visor** ['vaizə]：mask. **Philemon's roof**：据奥维德《变形记》，农夫(Philemon)在茅舍里热情招待微服下访的天神 Jove.

98 **thatched**：转义 whiskered.

101 **I would**：I wish. **did like**：did 为虚拟语气。

102 **So would not I**：I would not like you (so 代替 like you)。

114 **Amen** [,ɑ:'men]：基督教祈祷中的祝愿和附和语。

116 **is done!**：has finished. **clerk**：parish clerk who led the responses in church services.

121 **At a word**：in a word；briefly.

122 **waggling**：palsied motion，老人头微摇的症状。

123 **tell you true**：tell you the truth.

124 **do him so ill-well**：imitate his defect so well.

125 **dry**：dried or withered. **up and down**：all over.

130   Go to, mum, you are he. Graces will appear, and
there's an end.

        They step aside.

BEATRICE Will you not tell me who told you so?

BENEDICK No, you shall pardon me.

135   BEATRICE Nor will you not tell me who you are?

BENEDICK Not now.

BEATRICE That I was disdainful, and that I had my good
wit out of the 'Hundred Merry Tales'. Well, this was
Signior Benedick that said so.

140   BENEDICK What's he?

BEATRICE I am sure you know him well enough.

BENEDICK Not I, believe me.

BEATRICE Did he never make you laugh?

BENEDICK I pray you, what is he?

145   BEATRICE Why, he is the Prince's jester, a very dull
fool. Only his gift is in devising impossible slanders.
None but libertines delight in him; and the commendation is not in his wit, but in his villainy; for
he both pleases men and angers them, and then they

150   laugh at him and beat him. I am sure he is in the fleet.
I would he had boarded me.

BENEDICK When I know the gentleman, I'll tell him
what you say.

BEATRICE Do, do. He'll but break a comparison or

155   two on me; which peradventure, not marked or not
laughed at, strikes him into melancholy; and then
there's a partridge wing saved, for the fool will eat
no supper that night. [*Music.*] We must follow the
leaders.

160   BENEDICK In every good thing.

BEATRICE Nay, if they lead to any ill, I will leave them
at the next turning.

        Dance. Exeunt [*all but Don John,*

130 **Go to** 〈古语〉：No more of this，去你的吧。 **mum**：hush，no more talk. **Graces**：good qualities. **will appear**：总会显露出来。

131 **there's an end**：there's no more to be said about it.

137 **That … disdainful**：that 为引导宾语从句的连词(接 133 行的话，Will you not tell me who told you that I …?)

138 **'Hundred Merry Tales'**：a common jest-book first printed in 1525.

146 **Only his**：his only. **impossible**：incredible，absurd.

148 **villainy**：coarseness.

150—151 **fleet**：company of maskers. **boarded**：closed in on；(figuratively) accosted，addressed.

154 **comparison**：satirical simile. **break … comparison or**：tilt with words，crack a joke (比较 break a lance with，中世纪骑马持长矛对冲比武)。

155 **peradventure**：perhaps. **marked**：noticed.

157 **partridge wing**：鹌鹑翅膀(被认为是珍馐)。

159 **leaders**：the leading couple in the dance.

Borachio, and Claudio.

165 JOHN Sure my brother is amorous on Hero and hath
         withdrawn her father to break with him about it. The
         ladies follow her and but one visor remains.

     BORACHIO And that is Claudio. I know him by his
         bearing.

170 JOHN Are not you Signior Benedick?

     CLAUDIO You know me well. I am he.

     JOHN Signior, you are very near my brother in his
         love. He is enamored on Hero. I pray you dissuade
         him from her; she is no equal for his birth. You may

175   do the part of an honest man in it.

     CLAUDIO How know you he loves her?

     JOHN I heard him swear his affection.

     BORACHIO So did I too, and he swore he would marry
         her to-night.

180 JOHN Come, let us to the banquet.

                              Exeunt. Manet Claudio.

     CLAUDIO

     Thus answer I in name of Benedick
     But hear these ill news with the ears of Claudio.
     'Tis certain so. The Prince woos for himself.

185 Friendship is constant in all other things
     Save in the office and affairs of love.
     Therefore all hearts in love use their own tongues;
     Let every eye negotiate for itself
     And trust no agent; for beauty is a witch

190 Against whose charms faith melteth into blood.
     This is an accident of hourly proof,

     Which I mistrusted not. Farewell therefore Hero!
                    Enter Benedick.

     BENEDICK Count Claudio?

195 CLAUDIO Yea, the same.

     BENEDICK Come, will you go with me?

165 **Sure**：surely. **amorous on**：in love with.

167 **visor**：mask(这里是用服饰代替人的转喻 metonymy 用法,意指戴假面具的人)。

180 **Let us to**：Let us go to. **banquet**：a dessert of sweetmeats, fruit and wine, served separately as a refreshment after the dance.

181 *Manet* ['mɑːnet]〈拉丁语〉：remains,留在台上。

184 **certain**：certainly.

186 **office**：business.

190 **Against**：at, before. **charms**：magic power. **faith**：loyalty. **blood**：passion. **faith melteth into blood**："忠诚"熔化为"情欲"(正如巫婆熔化她所想消灭的人的蜡像一样)。

191 **accident of hourly proof**：happening seen every hour,司空见惯的事。

CLAUDIO Whither?

BENEDICK Even to the next willow, about your own business, County. What fashion will you wear the garland of? about your neck, like an usurer's chain? or under your arm, like a lieutenant's scarf? You must wear it one way, for the Prince hath got your Hero.

CLAUDIO I wish him joy of her.

BENEDICK Why, that's spoken like an honest drovier. So they sell bullocks. But did you think the Prince would have served you thus?

CLAUDIO I pray you leave me.

BENEDICK Ho! now you strike like the blind man! 'Twas the boy that stole your meat, and you'll beat the post.

CLAUDIO If it will not be, I'll leave you.   *Exit*.

BENEDICK Alas, poor hurt fowl! now will he creep into sedges. But, that my Lady Beatrice should know me, and not know me! The Prince's fool! Ha! it may be I go under that title because I am merry. Yea, but so I am apt to do myself wrong. I am not so reputed. It is the base (though bitter) disposition of Beatrice that puts the world into her person and so gives me out. Well, I'll be revenged as I may.

Enter the Prince [Don Pedro], Hero, Leonato.

PEDRO Now, signior, where's the Count? Did you see him?

BENEDICK Troth, my lord, I have played the part of Lady Fame. I found him here as melancholy as a lodge in a warren. I told him, and I think I told him true, that your grace had got the good will of this young lady, and I offered him my company to a willow tree, either to make him a garland, as be-

198 **Even**：just（为加强语气的副词）。 **willow**：通常为失恋的象征物。

199 **County**：count（用于称呼）。

200 **garland**：garland of willow. **chain**：gold chain，a symbol of wealth.

200—201 意思是，既然 Hero 为亲王所得，你可以向亲王索金以为补偿，或者向他挑战，进行决斗。 **lieutenant's scarf**：军官斜佩的肩带。

204 **wish him joy of her**：wish he will enjoy her（反话）。

205 **drovier**：drover，cattle trader.

206 **they**：people.

207 **served**：treated.

209—211 关于西班牙少年英雄 Lazarillo de Tormes 的故事，1586年有英译本出版。该少年偷了瞎眼睛主人的肉食，主人捉不住他，只能击柱出气。

212 **If it will not be**：if you will not leave me.

214 **sedges**：reeds. **that**：前省略 how unthinkable (or strange).

218 **bitter**：biting.

219—220 **puts the world into her person**：attributes to the world her own opinion. **gives me out**：reports me.

225 **Troth**：in faith.

226 **Lady Fame**：bearer of tidings，tale bearer.

227 **lodge in a warren**：小猎物（兔、雉等）繁殖围地内猎场看守人的小屋，孤寂而忧郁。

ing forsaken, or to bind him up a rod, as being worthy
to be whipt.

PEDRO To be whipt? What's his fault?

BENEDICK The flat transgression of a schoolboy who,
235 being overjoyed with finding a bird's nest, shows it his
companion, and he steals it.

PEDRO Wilt thou make a trust a transgression? The
transgression is in the stealer.

BENEDICK Yet it had not been amiss the rod had been
240 made, and the garland too; for the garland he might
have worn himself, and the rod he might have
bestowed on you, who, as I take it, have stolen his
bird's nest.

PEDRO I will but teach them to sing and restore them
245 to the owner.

BENEDICK If their singing answer your saying, by my
faith you say honestly.

PEDRO The Lady Beatrice hath a quarrel to you. The
gentleman that danced with her told her she is much
250 wronged by you.

BENEDICK O, she misused me past the endurance of a
block! An oak but with one green leaf on it would
have answered her; my very visor began to assume
life and scold with her. She told me, not thinking
255 I had been myself, that I was the Prince's jester,
that I was duller than a great thaw; huddling jest
upon jest with such impossible conveyance upon
me that I stood like a man at a mark, with a whole
army shooting at me. She speaks poniards, and ev-
260 ery word stabs. If her breath were as terrible as her
terminations, there were no living near her; she
would infect to the North Star. I would not marry
her though she were endowed with all that Adam
had left him before he transgressed. She would

231   **bind him up a rod**：为他扎一捆荆条。

233   **whipt**：whipped.

234   **flat**：plain.

236   **he**：his companion.

239—240   **it … made**：it would not have been wrong if the rod had been made.

244   **them**：the young birds in the nest.

246   **answer**：correspond with.

248   **quarrel to**：quarrel against, difference with.

250   **wronged**：slandered.

251—252   **misused**：abused.   **past … block!**：哪怕是一块木头，也会忍受不了。

254   **scold**：quarrel.

256   **thaw**：化雪。当时道路不好，化雪则泥泞难行，只好家居，生活枯燥。   **duller**：双关语 1.更傻笨；2.更枯燥乏味。

257   **impossible conveyance**：incredible jugglery.

258   **mark**：target.

261   **terminations**：terms, expressions, i. e., name-calling. **were**：would be.

262   **infect**：emit foul odors (supposed to carry infection).

263—264   **all that Adam had left him**：all that Adam had which had been left him (by God).《圣经·旧约·创世记》第 3 章，人类始祖亚当违背上帝之命被赶出乐园，这以前他是完善的。

265   have made Hercules have turned spit, yea, and
have cleft his club to make the fire too. Come, talk
not of her. You shall find her the infernal Ate in
good apparel. I would to God some scholar
would conjure her, for certainly, while she is here,
270   a man may live as quiet in hell as in a sanctuary; and
people sin upon purpose, because they would go
thither; so indeed all disquiet, horror, and perturba-
tion follows her.

       Enter Claudio and Beatrice.

275   PEDRO Look, here she comes.

    BENEDICK Will your grace command me any service to
the world's end? I will go on the slightest errand
now to the Antipodes that you can device to send
me on; I will fetch you a toothpicker now from the fur-
280   thest inch of Asia; bring you the length of Prester
John's foot; fetch you a hair off the great Cham's
beard; do you any embassage to the Pygmies — rather
than hold three words' conference with this harpy.
You have no employment for me?

285   PEDRO None, but to desire your good company.

    BENEDICK O God, sir, here's a dish I love not! I cannot
endure my Lady Tongue.   *Exit.*

    PEDRO Come, lady, come; you have lost the heart of Si-
gnior Benedick.

290   BEATRICE Indeed, my lord, he lent it me awhile, and
I gave him use for it — a double heart for his
single one. Marry, once before he won it of me
with false dice; therefore your grace may well say I
have lost it.

295   PEDRO You have put him down, lady; you have put him
down.

    BEATRICE So I would not he should do me, my lord,
lest I should prove the mother of fools. I have

265—266　**Hercules**：希腊传说中的大力英雄,他曾做利迪亚女王的奴隶,被迫穿女装,用纺锤纺纱。　**turned spit**：转动烤肉的铁钎,这是孩子都能做的事。　**yea**：yes.　**cleft his club**：劈开 Hercules 的大头木棍(他的武器)。　**have turned**：infinitive, perfect present.

267　**Ate** [ˈɑːti]：希腊神话中复仇和制造纠纷的女神。

268　**would to God**：prayed to God that.　**scholar**：懂拉丁语的学者,当时认为能驱魔。

269　**conjure her**：expel the evil spirits out of her.

269—273　When she is present, one will find the place so noisy that in comparison hell will be as quiet as a sanctuary to live in, so people will purposely commit sin in order to go to hell.

278　**Antipodes** [ænˈtipədiːz]：opposite side of the globe.

279　**toothpicker**：toothpick. 当时名贵的牙签用金、银制,饰以宝石,故要到亚洲去取。

280—281　**Prester John**：a legendary king, supposed to rule a Christian country in a remote part of Asia.

281—282　**Cham** [Kæm]：Khan [kɑːn] of Tartary [ˈtɑːtəri], ruler of the Mongols,蒙古族可汗,元朝皇帝。　**do…embassage** [ˈembəsidʒ]：serve as envoy.　**Pygmies**：传说住在印度或埃塞俄比亚的侏儒。

283　**conference**：conversation.　**harpy**：希腊神话中头部为女人,身翼为鸟的凶妖。这是指 Beatrice。

285　**but**：except.

286　**dish**：一道菜。

287　**Lady Tongue**：尖舌姑娘(这里指 Beatrice). tongue 牛舌,又是一道菜,这里是双关语。

288　**lost the heart**：won the heart(赢得爱情的反义语)。

291　**use**：interest；usury.　**double**：也作 deceitful 解。

293　**false dice**：掷骰子作弊。

295　**put him down**：put him to silence, get the better of him.

297　**do me**：put me down, throw me down (on a bed).

brought Count Claudio, whom you sent me to
300 seek.

PEDRO Why, how now, Count? Wherefore are you
sad?

CLAUDIO Not sad, my lord.

PEDRO How then? sick?

305 CLAUDIO Neither, my lord.

BEATRICE The Count is neither sad, nor sick, nor merry, nor well; but civil Count — civil as an orange, and
something of that jealous complexion.

PEDRO I' faith, lady, I think your blazon to be true;
310 though I'll be sworn, if he be so, his conceit is false.
Here, Claudio, I have wooed in thy name, and fair
Hero is won. I have broke with her father, and his
good will obtained. Name the day of marriage, and
God give thee joy!

315 LEONATO Count, take of me my daughter, and with her
my fortunes. His grace hath made the match, and all
grace say amen to it!

BEATRICE Speak, Count, 'tis your cue.

CLAUDIO Silence is the perfectest herald of joy. I were
320 but little happy if I could say how much. Lady, as you
are mine, I am yours. I give away myself for you and
dote upon the exchange.

BEATRICE Speak, cousin; or, if you cannot, stop his
mouth with a kiss and let not him speak neither.

325 PEDRO In faith, lady, you have a merry heart.

BEATRICE Yea, my lord; I thank it, poor fool, it keeps
on the windy side of care. My cousin tells him in his
ear that he is in her heart.

CLAUDIO And so she doth, cousin.

330 BEATRICE Good Lord, for alliance! Thus goes every one
to the world but I, and I am sunburnt. I may sit in a
corner and cry 'Heigh-ho for a husband!'

307   **civil**：和西班牙地名 Seville 谐音，当地产一种又甜又苦的橘子。

308   **jealous complexion**：yellow color，the color of jealousy.

309   **blazon**（纹章用语）：description.

310   **if he be so**：if he is jealous.   **conceit**：idea；conception（of what has happened）.

312   **broke with**：told.

315   **of**：from.

316—317   **all grace**：God，the source of all grace.

318   **cue**：演戏时的提示。   **'tis your cue**：该你上场或说话了。

319—320   **I were but**：I would only be.

321   **for**：in exchange for.

326   **poor fool**：poor dear（an expression of tenderness）.

327   **on the windy side of**：away from.

330—331   **for alliance**：Claudio has just called Beatrice cousin in anticipation of becoming her cousin by marriage (alliance).   **goes every one to the world**：everybody gets married.

331   **but**：except.   **sunburnt**：晒黑当时认为不美。

332   **'Heigh-ho for a husband!'**：the title of an old ballad.

PEDRO Lady Beatrice, I will get you one.

BEATRICE I would rather have one of your father's
335   getting. Hath your grace ne'er a brother like you?
Your father got excellent husbands, if a maid could
come by them.

PEDRO Will you have me, lady?

BEATRICE No, my lord, unless I might have another for
340   working days: your grace is too costly to wear every
day. But I beseech your grace pardon me. I was born
to speak all mirth and no matter.

PEDRO Your silence most offends me, and to be merry
best becomes you, for out o' question you were born
345   in a merry hour.

BEATRICE No, sure, my lord, my mother cried; but then
there was a star danced, and under that was I born.
Cousins, God give you joy!

LEONATO Niece, will you look to those things I told
350   you of?

BEATRICE I cry you mercy, uncle. By your grace's pardon.   *Exit Beatrice.*

PEDRO By my troth, a pleasant-spirited lady.

LEONATO There's little of the melancholy element in
355   her, my lord. She is never sad but when she sleeps,
and not ever sad then; for I have heard my daughter
say she hath often dreamt of unhappiness and waked
herself with laughing.

PEDRO She cannot endure to hear tell of a husband.

360 LEONATO O, by no means! She mocks all her wooers out
of suit.

PEDRO She were an excellent wife for Benedick.

LEONATO O Lord, my lord! if they were but a week
married, they would talk themselves mad.

365   PEDRO   County Claudio, when mean you to go to
church?

335 getting：begetting.

336 got excellent husbands：begot sons that could be excellent husbands.

340—341 your … day：拿衣服来打比的话，殿下太高贵了，不宜每天都穿着。

342 matter：substance（mirth 与 matter 有头韵）。

344 becomes：suits.

347 that：the dancing star.

348 Cousins：包括 Claudio 与 Hero，故用复数。

349 look to：see to, attend to.

351—352 cry you mercy：beg your pardon.   **By … pardon**：Please excuse me（addressed to the Prince）.

355 sad：serious. **but**：except.

356 ever：always.

359 endure to hear tell of：endure hearing people mention.

360—361 mocks … suit：makes fun of them until they quit wooing her.

362 were：would be.

365—366 go to church：go there to get married.

CLAUDIO To-morrow, my lord. Time goes on crutches till Love have all his rites.

LEONATO Not till Monday, my dear son, which is hence
370   a just sevennight; and a time too brief too, to have all things answer my mind.

PEDRO Come, you shake the head at so long a breathing; but I warrant thee, Claudio, the time shall not go dully by us. I will in the interim undertake
375   one of Hercules' labors, which is, to bring Signior Benedick and the Lady Beatrice into a mountain of affection th' one with th' other. I would fain have it a match, and I doubt not but to fashion it if you three will but minister such assistance as I shall
380   give you direction.

LEONATO My lord, I am for you, though it cost me ten nights' watchings.

CLAUDIO And I, my lord.

PEDRO And you too, gentle Hero?

385 HERO I will do any modest office, my lord, to help my cousin to a good husband.

PEDRO And Benedick is not the unhopefullest husband that I know. Thus far can I praise him: he is of a noble strain, of approved valor, and confirmed honesty. I will teach you how to humor your
390   cousin, that she shall fall in love with Benedick; and I, [*to Leonato and Claudio*] with your two helps, will so practice on Benedick that, in despite of his quick wit and his queasy stomach, he shall fall in love with Beatrice. If we can do this, Cupid
395   is no longer an archer; his glory shall be ours, for we are the only love-gods. Go in with me, and I will tell you my drift.   *Exit* [*with the others*].

367—368 Time … rites：喜事未办之前，时间就像拄着拐杖走路那样慢。 **have**：伊丽莎白时代条件或时间状语从句中常用虚拟语气一般式（即动词原形）。 **his**：its. **rites**：wedding ceremonies.

370 a just sevennight：exactly a week.

371 answer my mind：as I would like to have them.

372—373 breathing：delay.

375 Hercules' labors：希腊传说中大力英雄，曾被罚做十二件极难的事。

377 fain have：gladly make.

378 doubt not but to fashion it：doubt (fear) not about being prevented from bringing it about.

379 minister（v.）：give；render.

380 direction：instruction.

381 I am for you：I'll do your bidding.

382 watchings：loss of sleep.

385 modest：consistent with modesty.

386 to：to get.

387 unhopefullest：most unpromising.

388—389 strain：family；lineage. **approved**：tested. **confirmed**：steadfast.

389 humor（v.）：influence，affect the feelings of.

391—392 two helps：伊丽莎白时代抽象名词也可用复数。此例最明显，"你们俩人的帮助"成了 your two helps. **practice**：use stratagem.

392 despite：spite.

393 queasy stomach：delicate appetite.

394 Cupid：希腊神话中的爱神，眼盲，手执小弓箭，凡被他射中者即堕入情网。

397 drift：plan.

SCENE II

The house of Leonato

Enter [Don] John and Borachio.

JOHN It is so. The Count Claudio shall marry the daughter of Leonato.

BORACHIO Yea, my lord; but I can cross it.

JOHN Any bar, any cross, any impediment will be
5   medicinable to me. I am sick in displeasure to him, and
whatsoever comes athwart his affection ranges evenly
with mine. How canst thou cross this marriage?

BORACHIO Not honestly, my lord, but so covertly that
no dishonesty shall appear in me.

10   JOHN Show me briefly how.

BORACHIO I think I told your lordship, a year since, how
much I am in the favor of Margaret, the waiting gentlewoman to Hero.

JOHN I remember.

15   BORACHIO I can, at any unseasonable instant of the night,
appoint her to look out at her lady's chamber window.

JOHN What life is in that to be the death of this marriage?

BORACHIO The poison of that lies in you to temper.
Go you to the Prince your brother; spare not to
20   tell him that he hath wronged his honor in marrying the
renowned Claudio (whose estimation do you mightily
hold up) to a contaminated stale, such a one as Hero.

JOHN What proof shall I make of that?

BORACHIO Proof enough to misuse the Prince, to vex

II. ii

1 **shall**: is going to.

3 **cross**: obstruct; thwart.

4 **bar**: barrier.   **cross**: hindrance, interference.

5 **medicinable** [me'disinəbl]: healing; curative.   **sick in displeasure to**: loathingly displeased with.

6—7 **affection**: wish.   **ranges evenly with**: goes along with, meets.

11 **since**: ago.

15 **unseasonable instant**: exceptionally late time.

16 **appoint**: arrange for.

17 **life**: vitality, effect (life 与后面的 death 相对照)。

18 **temper**: mix, compound.

19 **spare not**: do not spare your effort.

21 **estimation**: worth, value.

22 **stale**: prostitute, harlot.

24 **misuse**: deceive, mislead.   **vex**: torment.

25   Claudio, to undo Hero, and kill Leonato. Look you for
       any other issue?

JOHN Only to despite them I will endeavor anything.

BORACHIO Go then; find me a meet hour to draw Don
       Pedro and the Count Claudio alone; tell them that
30   you know that Hero loves me; intend a kind of
       zeal both to the Prince and Claudio, as — in love
       of your brother's honor, who hath made this match,
       and his friend's reputation, who is thus like to be coz-
       ened with the semblance of a maid — that you have dis-
35   covered thus. They will scarcely believe this without
       trial. Offer them instances; which shall bear no less
       likelihood than to see me at her chamber window, hear
       me call Margaret Hero, hear Margaret term me Clau-
       dio; and bring them to see this the very night before
40   the intended wedding (for in) the meantime I will so
       fashion the matter that Hero shall be absent and there
       shall appear such seeming truth of Hero's disloyalty
       that jealousy shall be called assurance and all the prepa-
       ration overthrown.

45 JOHN Grow this to what adverse issue it can, I will put it
       in practice. Be cunning in the working this, and thy fee
       is a thousand ducats.

    BORACHIO Be you constant in the accusation, and my
       cunning shall not shame me.

    JOHN I will presently go learn their day of marriage.

                              Exit [with Borachio].

                           SCENE III

                     Leonato's orchard

                    Enter Benedick alone.

BENEDICK Boy!
           Enter Boy.

26 issue：outcome.

27 despite（v.）：spite.

28 meet hour：suitable time.

30 intend：pretend.

33—34 like（adv.）：likely.   **cozened**：deceived.   **semblance**：outward appearance.

36 trial：evidence.   **instances**：proofs.

37 likelihood：circumstantial evidence.

38 term（v.）：call, name.

43—44 jealousy：suspicion.   **assurance**：certainty.   **preparation**：preparations for the wedding.

45 Grow … can：No matter to what adverse issue（＝bad result）this may grow（＝develop）.

46 in the working this：在伊丽莎白时代，动名词前可加冠词，其后可带直接宾语，即不加 of.

47 ducats：一种金币。

49 shame me：make me ashamed.

50 presently：immediately.

BOY Signior?

BENEDICK In my chamber window lies a book. Bring it
    hither to me in the orchard.

5 BOY I am here already, sir.

BENEDICK I know that, but I would have thee hence and
    here again. *Exit [Boy].* I do much wonder that one
    man, seeing how much another man is a fool when he
    dedicates his behaviors to love, will, after he hath laughed
10 at such shallow follies in others, become the argument
    of his own scorn by falling in love; and such a man is
    Claudio. I have known when there was no music with
    him but the drum and the fife; and now had he rather
    hear the tabor and the pipe. I have known when he would
15 have walked ten mile afoot to see a good armor; and
    now will he lie ten nights awake carving the fashion of
    a new doublet. He was wont to speak plain and to the
    purpose, like an honest man and a soldier; and now is
    he turned orthography; his words are a very fantastical
20 banquet—just so many strange dishes. May I be so con-
    verted and see with these eyes? I cannot tell; I think not.
    I will not be sworn but love may transform me to an
    oyster; but I'll take my oath on it, till he have made an
    oyster of me he shall never make me such a fool. One
25 woman is fair, yet I am well; another is wise, yet I am
    well; another virtuous, yet I am well; but till all graces
    be in one woman, one woman shall not come in my grace.
    Rich she shall be, that's certain; wise, or I'll none; virtu-
    ous, or I'll never cheapen her; fair, or I'll never look on
30 her; mild, or come not near me; noble, or not I for an an-
    gel; of good discourse, an excellent musician, and her hair
    shall be of what color it please God. Ha, the Prince and
    Monsieur Love! [*retiring*] I will hide me in the arbor.

        Enter Prince [Don Pedro], Leonato, Claudio,
        Balthasar, with Music.

II. iii

2   Signior?：意大利语"先生"，现拼作 Signor.

4   orchard：garden.

5   I am here already：It is as good as done.

6   I know that：i. e., I know that you are here —— Benedick takes his words literally.

9   behaviors：acts and words.

10   argument：subject.

13   but the drum and the fife：i. e.,except military music.

14   the tabor and the pipe：small drum and reed instrument, associated with festivals and social gatherings.

15   armor：suit of armor.

16   carving：designing.

17—18   doublet：jacket.   **was wont to**：was accustomed to, used to.   **to the purpose**：to the point.

19   turned orthography：became a rhetorician.

20—21   converted：changed.

21   these eyes?：the eyes of a lover.

22   I will not be sworn but love may：I will not swear that love will not.

23   he：love（在这里拟人化了）。

24   oyster：牡蛎指死不开口的人，这刚好和 Benedick 的性格相反。

26   well：in good health, not affected.   **all graces**：all these good qualities：fairness, wisdom, virtue. 这些正是他承认 Beatrice 具备的优点，见 p. 70,211—213 行。

27   one woman shall not come in my grace：no woman will win my favor.

28   or I'll none：otherwise I'll have none.

29   cheapen：bargain for.

30—31   come not：she shall not come.   **noble，… angel**：她必须出身名门；否则，哪怕是个安琪儿我也不要。noble 和 angel 又是古时金币名称，在这里用作双关游戏。   **of good discourse**：skillful at reasoning and talking.

33   Monsieur Love!：指 Claudio.   **hide me**：hide myself.

PEDRO

    Come, shall we hear this music?

CLAUDIO

35   Yea, my good lord. How still the evening is,

    As hushed on purpose to grace harmony!

PEDRO

    See you where Benedick hath hid himself?

CLAUDIO

    O, very well, my lord. The music ended,

    We'll fit the kid-fox with a pennyworth.

PEDRO

40   Come, Balthasar, we'll hear that song again.

BALTHASAR

    O, good my lord, tax not so bad a voice

    To slander music any more than once.

PEDRO

    It is the witness still of excellency

    To put a strange face on his own perfection.

45   I pray thee sing, and let me woo no more.

BALTHASAR

    Because you talk of wooing, I will sing,

    Since many a wooer doth commence his suit

    To her he thinks not worthy, yet he woos,

    Yet will he swear he loves.

PEDRO   Nay, pray thee come;

50   Or if thou wilt hold longer argument,

    Do it in notes.

BALTHASAR   Note this before my notes:

    There's not a note of mine that's worth the noting.

PEDRO

    Why, these are very crotchets that he speaks!

    Note notes, forsooth, and nothing!   [*Music.*]

55 BENEDICK [*aside*] Now diving air! Now is his soul rav-

36 **As**: as if. **grace**: do honor to. **harmony**: melody, music.

38 **The music ended**（独立主格结构）: when the music is finished.

39 **fit … pennyworth**: give the sly young fellow what he deserves.

41 **tax not**: do not task, do not make demands upon.

42 **slander**: bring disgrace upon.

43 **the witness still of excellency**: always the evidence of excellence.

44 **put a strange face on**: pretend unfamiliarity with.

45 **woo**: beg, ask.

46 **wooing**: courting（"求婚"与前面的"请求"构成双关语）。

50 **argument**: talk, discourse.

51—52 **notes**: musical notes. **note … noting**: pay attention to this (i. e., my words) before I sing; there is not a musical note of mine that is worthy of notice（这里 note 为双关语 1. 音符; 2. 注意）。

53 **crotchets**: ①四分音符, small musical notes; ②strange fancies.

54 **Note … nothing!**: pay attention to your music and nothing else. **forsooth**（俗语）: in truth. **nothing**: 当时可读作 noting。

55 **air**: tune, melody. **his**: Balthasar's.

ished! Is it not strange that sheep's guts should hale
souls out of men's bodies? Well, a horn for my money, when all's done.

    [*Balthasar sings.*]

        The Song.

Sigh no more, ladies, sigh no more!
60   Men were deceivers ever,
One foot in sea, and one on shore;
   To one thing constant never.
     Then sigh not so,
     But let them go,
65   And be you blithe and bonny,
Converting all your sounds of woe
   Into Hey nonny, nonny.
Sing no more ditties, sing no moe,
   Of dumps so dull and heavy!
70   The fraud of men was ever so,
   Since summer first was leavy.
    Then sigh not so, etc.

PEDRO By my troth, a good song.

BALTHASAR And an ill singer, my lord.

75 PEDRO Ha, no, no, faith! Thou sing'st well enough for
a shift.

BENEDICK [*aside*] An he had been a dog that should have
howled thus, they would have hanged him; and I pray
God his bad voice bode no mischief. I had as live have
80 heard the night raven, come what plague could have
come after it.

PEDRO Yea, marry. Dost thou hear, Balthasar? I pray
thee get us some excellent music; for to-morrow night
we would have it at the Lady Hero's chamber window.

85 BALTHASAR The best I can, my lord.

PEDRO Do so. Farewell. *Exit Balthasar* [*with Musicians*]. Come hither, Leonato. What was it you told me

56   **sheep's guts**: strings，琴弦。The music is provided by a stringed instrument, probably a lute.   **hale**: draw.

57   **horn**: which sounds to war or to the hunt, is preferred by Benedick.

58   **when … done**: when all is said and done.

61   **One … shore**: like a sailor who leaves wife and mistresses behind on shore.

65   **blithe and bonny**: gay and cheerful（两词既同义又有头韵）。

67   **Hey nonny, nonny**: sounds denoting merriment.

68   **ditties**: short, simple songs.   **moe**: more.

69   **dumps**: sad songs, usually love songs.

70   **fraud**: deceitful behavior.

71   **leavy** (adj.): full of leaves.

75—76   **for a shift**: as a makeshift, for want of someone better. **shift**: emergency.

77   **An**: if.

79   **bode**: forbode.   **had as live**: had as lief, had rather.

80—81   **night raven**: 夜啼鸟（一种老鸦），portent of disaster. **come … it**: no matter what plague that could have come after it may come to me.

of today? that your niece Beatrice was in love with Signior Benedick?

90   CLAUDIO   O, ay! — [*aside to Pedro*] Stalk on, stalk on;
the fowl sits. — I did never think that lady would have
loved any man.

LEONATO   No, nor I neither; but most wonderful that
she should so dote on Signior Benedick, whom she hath

95   in all outward behaviors seemed ever to abhor.

BENEDICK   [*aside*] Is't possible? Sits the wind in that
corner?

LEONATO   By my troth, my lord, I cannot tell what to
think of it, but that she loves him with an enraged
affection, it is past the infinite of thought.

100 PEDRO   May be she doth but counterfeit.

CLAUDIO   Faith, like enough.

LEONATO   O God, counterfeit? There was never counterfeit of passion came so near the life of passion as she
discovers it.

105 PEDRO   Why, what effects of passion shows she?

CLAUDIO   [*aside*] Bait the hook well! This fish will bite.

LEONATO   What effects, my lord? She will sit you — you
heard my daughter tell you how.

CLAUDIO   She did indeed.

110 PEDRO   How, how, I pray you? You amaze me. I would
have thought her spirit had been invincible against all
assaults of affection.   .

LEONATO   I would have sworn it had, my lord — especially against Benedick.

115 BEATRICE   [*aside*] I should think this a gull but that the
white-bearded fellow speaks it. Knavery cannot, sure,
hide himself in such reverence.

CLAUDIO   [*aside*] He hath ta'en th' infection. Hold it
up.

PEDRO   Hath she made her affection known to Benedick?

88   **of**：about.   **that**：引导的名词从句与 it 同位。

90   **Stalk on**：step forward stealthily (alluding to a stalking-horse, a tame beast made to walk slowly near to wild fowl concealing the approach of the hunter, who keeps behind it).

91   **the fowl sits**：意为 Benedick stays there to be duped.

96   **Sits ... corner?**：Is that how things stand?

98—99   **but**：except.   **enraged**：frenzied, passionate.   **infinite**：furthest reach.

101   **like**：likely.

103   **came**：前省略 which.

104   **discovers**：reveals.

107   **She will sit you**：you 在这里为泛指的人称与格,仅加强语气,等于 She will sit, note this!

113   **it had**：her spirit had been invincible.

115   **gull**：trick, hoax.   **but that**：if ... not.

118   **ta'en**：taken.   **Hold it up**：keep it going.

120 LEONATO No,and swears she never will. That's her tor-
         ment.

     CLAUDIO ' Tis true indeed. So your daughter says.
         'Shall I,' says she, 'that have so oft encountered him
         with scorn, write to him that I love him?'

     LEONATO This says she now when she is beginning to
125   write to him; for she'll be up twenty times a night,
         and there will she sit in her smock till she have writ a
         sheet of paper. My daughter tells us all.

     CLAUDIO Now you talk of a sheet of paper, I remember a
         pretty jest your daughter told us of.

130 LEONATO O, when she had writ it, and was reading it
         over, she found 'Benedick' and 'Beatrice' between the
         sheet?

     CLAUDIO That.

     LEONATO O, she tore the letter into a thousand half-
135   pence, railed at herself that she should be so im-
         modest to write to one that she knew would flout her.
         'I measure him,' says she, 'by my own spirit; for I
         should flout him if he writ to me. Yea, though I love
         him, I should. '

140 CLAUDIO Then down upon her knees she falls, weeps,
         sobs, beats her heart, tears her hair, prays, curses
         — 'O sweet Benedick! God give me patience!'

     LEONATO She doth indeed; my daughter says so. And
         the ecstasy hath so much overborne her that my daugh-
145   ter is sometime afeard she will do a desperate outrage
         to herself. It is very true.

     PEDRO It were good that Benedick knew of it by some
         other, if she will not discover it.

     CLAUDIO To what end? He would make but a sport of it
150   and torment the poor lady worse.

     PEDRO An he should, it were an alms to hang him!
         She's an excellent sweet lady, and (out of all suspicion)

122 **encountered**：confronted.

126 **smock**：chemise.   **writ**：written.

131—132 **between the sheet?**：in the folded sheet of paper，with pun on bedsheets.

134—135 **halfpence**：tiny pieces.

136 **flout**：mock.

144 **ecstasy**：excess of passion，madness.   **overborne**：overwhelmed.

145 **afeard**：afraid.   **outrage**：violent act 指自杀。

147 **were**：would be.

148 **discover**：reveal.

151 **An**：if.   **an alms**：a deed of charity，a good deed.

152 (**out of all suspicion**)：beyond doubt.

she is virtuous.

CLAUDIO And she is exceeding wise.

155 PEDRO In everything but in loving Benedick.

LEONATO O, my lord, wisdom and blood combating in so tender a body, we have ten proofs to one that blood hath the victory. I am sorry for her, as I have just cause, being her uncle and her guardian.

160 PEDRO I would she had bestowed this dotage on me. I would have daffed all other respects and made her half myself. I pray you tell Benedick of it and hear what 'a will say.

LEONATO Were it good, think you?

165 CLAUDIO Hero thinks surely she will die; for she says she will die if he love her not, and she will die ere she make her love known, and she will die, if he woo her, rather than she will bate one breath of her accustomed crossness.

170 PEDRO She doth well. If she should make tender of her love, 'tis very possible he'll scorn it; for the man (as you know all) hath a contemptible spirit.

CLAUDIO He is a very proper man.

PEDRO He hath indeed a good outward happiness.

175 CLAUDIO Before God! and in my mind, very wise.

PEDRO He doth indeed show some sparks that are like wit.

CLAUDIO And I take him to be valiant.

PEDRO As Hector, I assure you; and in the managing of quarrels you may say he is wise, for either he avoids

180 them with great discretion, or undertakes them with a most Christianlike fear.

LEONATO If he do fear God, 'a must necessarily keep peace. If he break the peace, he ought to enter into a quarrel with fear and trembling.

185 PEDRO And so will he do; for the man doth fear God, howsoever it seems not in him by some large jests he

154　**exceeding**（adv.）：exceedingly.

156　**blood**：passion.

159　**guardian**：Beatrice 有监护人,这说明她是孤女。

160　**dotage**：doting affection,痴情。

161—162　**daffed all other respects**：doffed（put aside）all other considerations（such as the difference of rank）.　**half myself**：my better-half.

162　**'a**：he.

168—169　**bate**：abate.　**crossness**：inclination to quarrel.

170　**make tender of**：make an offer of.

172　**contemptible**：contemptuous, scornful.

173　**proper**：handsome.

174　**good outward happiness**：attractive appearance.

176　**wit**：intelligence.

178　**Hector**：荷马史诗《伊利亚特》中特洛伊方面最英勇善战的王子,但另一意思是虚张声势者。

181　**Christianlike fear**：dread and reverence of God.

186　**by**：to judge by.　**large**：coarse.

will make. Well, I am sorry for your niece. Shall we
go seek Benedick and tell him of her love?

CLAUDIO Never tell him, my lord. Let her wear it out
190 with good counsel.

LEONATO Nay, that's impossible; she may wear her
heart out first.

PEDRO Well, we will hear further of it by your daughter.
Let it cool the while. I love Benedick well, and I could
195 with he would modestly examine himself to see how
much he is unworthy so good a lady.

LEONATO My lord, will you walk? Dinner is ready.

They walk away.

CLAUDIO If he do not dote on her upon this, I will never
trust my expectation.

200 PEDRO Let there be the same net spread for her, and that
must your daughter and her gentlewomen carry. The
sport will be, when they hold one an opinion of another's dotage, and no such matter. That's the scene that
I would see, which will be merely a dumb show. Let
205 us send her to call him in to dinner.

Exeunt Don Pedro, Claudio, and Leonato.

BENEDICK [*advancing*] This can be no trick. The conference was sadly borne; they have the truth of this from
Hero; they seem to pity the lady. It seems her affec-
tions have their full bent. Love me? Why, it must be
210 requited. I hear how I am censured. They say I will
bear myself proudly if I perceive the love come from
her. They say too that she will rather die then give any
sign of affection. I did never think to marry. I must
not seem proud. Happy are they that hear their detrac-
215 tions and can put them to mending. They say the lady
is fair — 'tis a truth, I can bear them witness; and virtuous — 'tis so, I cannot reprove it; and wise, but for
loving me — by my troth, it is no addition to her wit,

189 wear it out: get over it.

190 counsel: consideration, reflection.

194 the while: for the time being.

198 upon: as a result of.

201 carry: manage.

202—203 sport: fun, joke. **they … dotage**: each of them thinks the other is in love. **no such matter**: there's nothing of the sort.

204 dumb show: pantomime, 哑剧(因为他们在一起时,不会再像过去那样唇枪舌剑了)。

206—207 conference: conversation. **sadly borne**: seriously carried on.

208—209 her … bent: her emotions are tightly stretched, like a bow fully bent.

211 bear myself proudly: put on airs.

213 think to marry: think of marrying.

214—215 their detractions: criticism of their faults. **put them to mending**: correct them.

217 reprove: disprove. **but**: except.

nor no great argument of her folly, for I will be horri-
220   bly in love with her. I may chance have some odd
quirks and remnants of wit broken on me because I
have railed so long against marriage. But doth not the
appetite alter? A man loves the meat in his youth that
he cannot endure in his age. Shall quips and sentences
225   and these paper bullets of the brain awe a man from the
career of his humor? No, the world must be peopled.
When I said I would die a bachelor, I did not think I
should live till I were married. Here comes Beatrice.
By this day, she's a fair lady! I do spy some marks of
230   love in her.

　　　　Enter Beatrice.

BEATRICE Against my will I am sent to bid you come in
to dinner.

BENEDICK Fair Beatrice, I thank you for your pains.

BEATRICE I took no more pains for those thanks than you
235   take pains to thank me. If it had been painful, I would
not have come.

BENEDICK You take pleasure then in the message?

BEATRICE Yea, just so much as you may take upon a
knive's point, and choke a daw withal. You have no
240   stomach, signior. Fare you well.   *Exit.*

BENEDICK Ha! 'Against my will I am sent to bid you
come in to dinner. ' There's a double meaning in that.
'I took no more pains for those thanks than you took
pains to thank me. ' That's as much as to say, 'Any
245   pains that I take for you is as easy as thanks. ' If I do
not take pity of her, I am a villain; if I do not love her,

I am a Jew. I will go get her picture.   *Exit.*

219—220　argument：proof.　　**horribly**：madly.　　**chance**：perhaps.　　**odd**：misapplied.

221　quirks：quips.

224　sentences：epigrams，wise sayings.

226　career of his humor：course of his inclination.

229　By this day：表强调的赌咒语，等于 I swear by this day.

233　pains：trouble. 此句为 Benedick 第一次用素体韵文，表明他情感的改变。

235　pains：双关语 1. trouble；2. 痛苦。

239—240　daw：jackdaw，寒鸦（转意为傻瓜）。　　**withal**：with. **You have no stomach**：you have no appetite（for repartee）.

247　Jew：no Christian.

ACT III

SCENE I

Leonato's orchard

*Enter Hero and two Gentlewomen, Margaret
and Ursula.*

HERO

    Good Margaret, run thee to the parlor.
    There shalt thou find my cousin Beatrice
    Proposing with the Prince and Claudio.
    Whisper her ear and tell her, I and Ursula
5   Walk in the orchard, and our whole discourse
    Is all of her. Say that thou overheard'st us;
    And did her steal into the pleachèd bower,
    Where honeysuckles, ripened by the sun,
    Forbid the sun to enter — like favorites,
10   Made proud by princes, that advance their pride
    Against that power that bred it. There will she hide her
    To listen our propose. This is thy office.
    Bear thee well in it and leave us alone.

MARGARET

    I'll make her come, I warrant you, presently. [*Exit.*]

HERO

15   Now, Ursula, when Beatrice doth come,
    As we do trace this alley up and down,
    Our talk must only be of Benedick.
    When I do name him, let it be thy part
    To praise him more than ever man did merit.
20   My talk to thee must be how Benedick
    Is sick in love with Beatrice. Of this matter

III. i

   1 **thee**：在命令句中，thou 改为 thee.

   3 **Proposing**：conversing, talking.

   4 **Whisper her ear**：Whisper in her ear.   **Ursula**：Ursley 的爱称。

   7 **pleachèd**：entwined (with vines).

   8 **ripened**：brought to full growth.

   9 **favorites**：宠臣。

   10 **advance**：raise, lift up.

   12 **listen our propose**：listen to our conversation.   **office**：business, task.

   13 **Bear ··· it**：do it well.

   14 **presently**：immediately.

   16 **trace**：tread, walk along.

   18 **part**：role.

   21 **this matter**：指 love.

Is little Cupid's crafty arrow made,
That only wounds by hearsay.

     Enter Beatrice [and hides].

Now begin;
For look where Beatrice like a lapwing runs
25   Close by the ground, to hear our conference.

URSULA

The pleasant'st angling is to see the fish
Cut with her golden oars the silver stream
And greedily devour the treacherous bait.
So angle we for Beatrice, who even now
30   Is couchèd in the woodbine coverture.
Fear you not my part of the dialogue.

HERO

Then go we near her, that her ear lose nothing
Of the false sweet bait that we lay for it.

    They move.

No, truly, Ursula, she is too disdainful.
35   I know her spirits are as coy and wild
As haggards of the rock.

URSULA   But are you sure
That Benedick loves Beatrice so entirely?

HERO

So says the Prince, and my new-trothèd lord.

URSULA

And did they bid you tell her of it, madam?

HERO

40   They did entreat me to acquaint her of it;
But I persuaded them, if they loved Benedick,
To wish him wrestle with affection
And never to let Beatrice know of it.

URSULA

Why did you so? Doth not the gentleman
45   Deserve as full as fortunate a bed
As ever Beatrice shall couch upon?

24 **lapwing**：田凫。

27 **oars**：指 fins.

30 **couchèd**：hidden.   **woodbine coverture**：honeysuckle shelter.

32 **go we**：let's go.

36 **haggards**：悍鹰。

37 **entirely**：sincerely.

38 **new-trothèd**：newly-betrothed.

42 **To... wrestle with**：struggle with，try to overcome.

45 **as full**：fully.

45—46 deserve a wife every bit as good as Beatrice.

HERO

O god of love! I know he doth deserve
As much as may be yielded to a man;
But Nature never framed a woman's heart
50   Of prouder stuff than that of Beatrice.
Disdain and scorn ride sparkling in her eyes,
Misprizing what they look on; and her wit
Values itself so highly that to her
All matter else seems weak. She cannot love,
55   Nor take no shape nor project of affection,
She is so self-endeared.

URSULA   Sure I think so;
And therefore certainly it were not good
She knew his love, lest she'll make sport at it.

HERO

Why, you speak truth. I never yet saw man,
60   How wise, how noble, young, how rarely featured,
But she would spell him backward. If fair-faced,
She would swear the gentleman should be her sister;
If black, why, Nature, drawing of an antic,
Made a foul blot; if tall, a lance ill-headed;
65   If low, an agate very vilely cut;
If speaking, why, a vane blown with all winds;
If silent, why, a block movèd with none.
So turns she every man the wrong side out
And never gives to truth and virtue that
70   Which simpleness and merit purchaseth.

URSULA

Sure, sure, such carping is not commendable.

HERO

No, not to be so odd, and from all fashions,
As Beatrice is, cannot be commendable.
But who dare tell her so? If I should speak,
75   She would mock me into air; O, she would laugh me

52 **Misprizing**：mistaking，undervaluing.

54 **weak**：worthless.

55 **Nor … no**：莎士比亚时代常用两个否定词来表示一个强调的否定。 **project**：conception，idea. **take … affection**：accept any form or idea of love from another.

56 **self-endeared**：in love with herself.

58 **make sport at it**：make fun of it.

60 **How**：however. **rarely**：finely.

61 **But**：that … not. **spell him backward**：misrepresent him, describe him in a perverse way. **fair-faced**：of a white complexion.

63 **drawing of**：drawing. **antic**：grotesque figure，buffoon.

64 **lance ill-headed**：spear with an ill-proportioned point.

65 **agate**：玛瑙。 **vilely**：badly (The allusion is to the tiny human figures often cut in agate, used as seals).

66 **speaking**：talkative. **vane**：weather vane，风向标。 **with**：by.

67 **block**：block of wood or stone. **none**：no wind.

68 **turns … every man the wrong side out**：与 61 行 spell him backward 同义。

70 **simpleness**：integrity. **purchaseth**：deserves.

71 **carping**：faultfinding，吹毛求疵。

72 **not**：仅仅是重复 cannot 的否定意义，在现代英语中应该去掉。 **odd**：singular，peculiar. **from**：contrary to.

75 **into air**：to death.

Out of myself, press me to death with wit!
Therefore let Benedick, like covered fire,
Consume away in sighs, waste inwardly.
It were a better death than die with mocks,
80   Which is as bad as die with tickling.

URSULA

Yet tell her of it. Hear what she will say.

HERO

No; rather I will go to Benedick
And counsel him to fight against his passion.
And truly, I'll devise some honest slanders
85   To stain my cousin with. One doth not know
How much an ill word may empoison liking.

URSULA

O, do not do your cousin such a wrong!
She cannot be so much without true judgment
(Having so swift and excellent a wit
90   As she is prized to have) as to refuse
So rare a gentleman as Signior Benedick.

HERO

He is the only man of Italy,
Always excepted my dear Claudio.

URSULA

I pray you be not angry with me, madam,
95   Speaking my fancy: Signior Benedick,
For shape, for bearing argument, and valor,
Goes foremost in report through Italy.

HERO

Indeed he hath an excellent good name.

URSULA

His excellence did earn it ere he had it.
100   When are you married, madam?

HERO

Why, every day to-morrow! Come, go in.

76 Out of myself: to death.   **press me to death**: This alludes to a punishment of placing more and more heavy weights on the chest of a criminal until he confesses or dies.

78 Consume away: waste away.

79, 80 with: by.

84 honest: decent, innocent.

86 empoison: poison.

90 prized: esteemed.

92 only: one and only, foremost, best.

93 excepted … Claudio: with Claudio excepted(原文系独立主格结构)。

95 Speaking my fancy: if I speak precisely as I think.

96 argument: intelligent conversation.

97 report: reputation.

98 name: fame.

100 married: going to be married.

101 every day to-morrow: tomorrow and for ever after.

I'll show thee some attires, and have thy counsel
Which is the best to furnish me to-morrow.

  They walk away.

URSULA

She's limed, I warrant you! We have caught her, madam.
HERO

105 If it prove so, then loving goes by haps;
Some Cupid kills with arrows, some with traps.

         Exeunt Hero and Ursula.

BEATRICE *coming forth from hiding*

What fire is in mine ears? Can this be true?
 Stand I condemned for pride and scorn so much?
Contempt, farewell! And maiden pride, adieu!
110 No glory lives behind the back of such.
And, Benedick, love on; I will requite thee,
 Taming my wild heart to thy loving hand.
If thou dost love, my kindness shall incite thee
 To bind our loves up in a holy band;
115 For others say thou dost deserve, and I
Believe it better than reportingly.   *Exit.*

SCENE II

The house of Leonato

Enter Prince [Don Pedro], Claudio,
Benedick, and Leonato.

PEDRO I do but stay till your marriage be consummate,
 and then go I toward Arragon.

CLAUDIO I'll bring you thither, my lord, if you'll
 vouchsafe me.

5 PEDRO Nay, that would be as great a soil in the new
 gloss of your marriage as to show a child his new coat
 and forbid him to wear it. I will only be bold with Ben-

102 **attires**：head-dresses.

103 **furnish**：adorn.

104 **limed**：caught with birdlime.

105 **haps**：chance.

107 **What** ... **ears**?：How my ears burn! (It's believed that one's ears burn when one is talked about behind his back.) Beatrice 以前都讲道白,这里她突转诗体,说明感情的变化。这里的十行诗韵脚为 a b a b c d c d e e.

110 **No ... such**：no praise is expected behind the backs of scornful and proud persons.

112 **Taming ... hand**：She picks up the hawk image of lines 35—36 above. **to**：at.

113 **kindness**：affection, tenderness.

114 **loves**：抽象名词的复数。 **band**：ties of marriage.

116 **reportingly**：by hearsay.

III. ii

1 **consummate**：consummated.

4 **vouchsafe**：allow, permit.

5 **soil**：blemish, stain.

6 **gloss**：lustre of the surface.

7 **be bold with**：be so bold as to ask.

edick for his company; for, from the crown of his head
to the sole of his foot, he is all mirth. He hath twice or
thrice cut Cupid's bowstring, and the little hangman

10   dare not shoot at him. He hath a heart as sound as a
bell; and his tongue is the clapper, for what his heart
thinks, his tongue speaks.

BENEDICK   Gallants, I am not as I have been.

LEONATO   So say I. Methinks you are sadder.

15   CLAUDIO   I hope he be in love.

PEDRO   Hang him, truant! There's no true drop of blood
in him to be truly touched with love. If he be sad, he
wants money.

BENEDICK   I have the toothache.

20   PEDRO   Draw it.

BENEDICK   Hang it!

CLAUDIO   You must hang it first and draw it afterwards.

PEDRO   What? sigh for the toothache?

LEONATO   Where is but a humor or a worm.

25   BENEDICK   Well, every one can master a grief but he that
has it.

CLAUDIO   Yet say I he is in love.

PEDRO   There is no appearance of fancy in him, unless it
be a fancy that he hath to strange disguises; as to be a

30   Dutchman to-day, a Frenchman to-morrow; or in the
shape of two countries at once, as a German from the
waist downward, all slops, and a Spaniard from the hip
upward, no doublet. Unless he have a fancy to this
foolery, as it appears he hath, he is no fool for fancy,

35   as you would have it appear he is.

CLAUDIO   If he be not in love with some woman, there is
no believing old signs. 'A brushes his hat o' mornings. What should that bode?

PEDRO   Hath any man seen him at the barber's?

40   CLAUDIO   No, but the barber's man hath been seen with

9   **little hangman**：rascal (指 Cupid).

13   **Gallants**：哥儿们。

14   **sadder**：more serious.

16   **Hang him, truant!**：Hang him for a tramp (in love)!

20   **Draw**：pull out.

21   **Hang it!**：an expression of disappointment or mild despair, 真是要命。

22   **draw**：cut out the entrails (内脏) of. This is a punning allusion to the old punishment of criminals who were first hanged and then drawn.

24   **Where**：where there.   **but**：only.   **humor**：body fluid, rheum.

25   **master**：overcome, control.   **grief**：physical or mental pain.   **but**：except.

28   **fancy**：love.

29   **fancy**：whim (与上一行的 fancy 构成双关语)。   **disguises**：clothes.

32   **slops**：loose breeches, 灯笼裤。

33   **doublet**：旧时英国式上装。

34   **fool for fancy**：lover.

37—38   **old signs**：symptoms traditionally believed in.   **'A**：he.   **o'mornings**：of mornings, some time every morning.   **bode**：forebode, portend.

him, and the old ornament of his cheek hath already
stuffed tennis balls.

LEONATO Indeed he looks younger than he did, by the
loss of a beard.

45 PEDRO Nay, 'a rubs himself with civet. Can you smell
him out by that?

CLAUDIO That's as much as to say, the sweet youth's in
love.

PEDRO The greatest note of it is his melancholy.

CLAUDIO And when was he wont to wash his face?

50 PEDRO Yea, or to paint himself? for the which I hear
what they say of him.

CLAUDIO Nay, but his jesting spirit, which is now crept
into a lutestring, and now governed by stops.

PEDRO Indeed that tells a heavy tale for him. Conclude,

55 conclude, he is in love.

CLAUDIO Nay, but I know who loves him.

PEDRO That would I know too. I warrant, one that
knows him not.

CLAUDIO Yes, and his ill conditions; and in despite of

60 all, dies for him.

PEDRO She shall be buried with her face upwards.

BENEDICK Yet is this no charm for the toothache. Old signior, walk aside with me. I have studied eight or nine
wise words to speak to you, which these hobbyhorses
must not hear.

65   *Exeunt Benedick and Leonato.*

PEDRO For my life, to break with him about Beatrice!

CLAUDIO 'Tis even so. Hero and Margaret have by this
played their parts with Beatrice, and then the two
bears will not bite one another when they meet.

Enter John the Bastard.

70 JOHN My lord and brother, God save you.

PEDRO Good den, brother.

41 **ornament of his cheek**：his beard.

45 **Nay**：moreover.   **civet**：a perfume from the civet cat（香猫）。

47 **sweet**：双关语 1. 香的；2. 性情可爱的。

48 **note**：mark，sign.

49 **was…wont to**：used to.

50 **paint himself?**：use cosmetics.

52 **is…crept**：has crept.

53 **stops**：lute（类似琵琶的手指按圈）。

54 **heavy**：sorry.

56 **Nay**：indeed.

58 **knows**：understands.

59 **ill conditions**：bad qualities.   **despite**：spite.

60 **dies**：双关语 1. wastes away；2. comes to orgasm，pines for.

61 **She … upwards**：双关语 1. She will be buried like a Christian；
2. She will be smothered by Benedick.

62 **charm**：cure.   **Old**：a term of respect.

63 **studied**：considered，pondered.

64 **hobby horses**：buffoons.

66 **For my life**：upon my life.   **to break with**：to make a disclo-
sure to.

67 **by this**：by this time.

71 **Good den**：good e'en，good evening.

JOHN   If your leisure served, I would speak with you.

PEDRO   In private?

JOHN   If it please you. Yet Count Claudio may hear, for
75   what I would speak of concerns him.

PEDRO   What's the matter?

JOHN   [*to Claudio*] Means your lordship to be married to-
        morrow?

PEDRO   You know he does.

80   JOHN   I know not that, when he knows what I know.

CLAUDIO   If there be any impediment, I pray you discover
        it.

JOHN   You may think I love you not. Let that appear
        hereafter, and aim better at me by that I now will man-
        ifest. For my brother, I think he holds you well and in
85   dearness of heart hath holp to effect your ensuing mar-
        riage — surely suit ill spent and labor ill bestowed!

PEDRO   Why, what's the matter?

JOHN   I came hither to tell you, and, circumstances
        shortened (for she has been too long a-talking of), the
90   lady is disloyal.

CLAUDIO   Who? Hero?

JOHN   Even she — Leonato's Hero, your Hero, every
        man's Hero.

CLAUDIO   Disloyal?

95   JOHN   The word is too good to paint out her wickedness.
        I could say she were worse; think you of a worse title,
        and I will fit her to it. Wonder not till further warrant.
        Go but with me to-night, you shall see her chamber
        window entered, even the night before her wedding
100   day. If you love her then, to-morrow wed her. But it
        would better fit your honor to change your mind.

CLAUDIO   May this be so?

PEDRO   I will not think it.

JOHN   If you dare not trust that you see, confess not that

72   **If ... served**: if you have time.

80   **I ... that**: I don't know that, I am not so sure about that.

81   **discover**: reveal.

82—83   **Let ... hereafter**: let me be judged hereafter, not now.

83—84   **aim better at me**: judge better of me.   **that**: what. **manifest**: reveal.   **For**: as for.   **holds you well**: likes you very much.

85   **dearness of heart**: friendship.   **holp**: helped.

88—89   **circumstances shortened**: with all unnecessary detail omitted（原文为独立主格结构）。   **a-talking of**: talked about.

90   **disloyal**: unfaithful.

95   **paint out**: portray.

97   **warrant**: proof.

103   **think it**: think of it, believe it.

104   **that**: what.   **confess**: admit.

105   you know. If you will follow me, I will show you
       enough; and when you have seen more and heard
       more, proceed accordingly.

    CLAUDIO If I see anything to-night why I should not mar-
       ry her to-morrow, in the congregation where I should
110   wed there will I shame her.

    PEDRO And, as I wooed for thee to obtain her, I will join
       with thee to disgrace her.

    JOHN I will disparage her no farther till you are my wit-
       nesses. Bear it coldly but till midnight, and let the issue
115   show itself.

    PEDRO O day untowardly turned!

    CLAUDIO O mischief strangely thwarting!

    JOHN O plague right well prevented!
       So will you say when you have seen the sequel.

                                          [*Exeunt.*]

SCENE III

A Street in Messina

Enter Dogberry and his compartner
[*Verges*], *with the Watch.*

    DOGBERRY Are you good men and true?

    VERGES Yea, or else it were pity but they should suffer
       salvation, body and soul.

    DOGBERRY Nay, that were a punishment too good for
5   them if they should have any allegiance in them, being
       chosen for the Prince's watch.

    VERGES Well, give them their charge, neighbor Dogberry.

    DOGBERRY First, who think you the most desartless man
       to be constable?

10 1. WATCH Hugh Oatcake, sir, or George Seacole, for
       they can write and read.

108   why：about why，to prove why.

109   congregation：gathering in church.

110   shame：humiliate.

114   coldly：coolly，patiently.

116   untowardly：unluckily.

118   plague：misfortune.

III. iii

compartner：partner，here deputy constable，警佐。   *the Watch*：night watchmen.

2—3   but：that … not.   **salvation**：Dogberry 和他的同伴都是些不学无术的人，却喜欢用大字眼，常常误用了词的反义词，造成了很多笑料。如这里他把 salvation 当作 damnation(下地狱)的意思来用。

5   allegiance(忠诚)：被 Dogberry 当作 treachery(不忠)。

7   charge：instructions.

8   desartless（＝desertless 要不得）：被 Dogberry 当作 deserving (称职的)。

10   1. WATCH：the first watchman，下类推。

DOGBERRY   Come hither, neighbor Seacole. God hath
    blessed you with a good name. To be a well-favored
    man is the gift of fortune, but to write and read comes
    by nature.

15 2. WATCH   Both which, master constable —

DOGBERRY   You have. I knew it would be your answer.
    Well, for your favor, sir, why, give God thanks and
    make no boast of it; and for your writing and reading,
    let that appear when there is no need of such vanity.

20   You are thought here to be the most senseless and fit
    man for the constable of the watch. Therefore bear you
    the lanthorn. This is your charge: you shall compre-
    hend all vagrom men; you are to bid any man stand, in
    the Prince's name.

25 2. WATCH   How if 'a will not stand?

DOGBERRY   Why then, take no note of him, but let him
    go, and presently call the rest of the watch together
    and thank God you are rid of a knave.

VERGES   If he will not stand when he is bidden, he is
30   none of the Prince's subjects.

DOGBERRY   True, and they are to meddle with none but
    the Prince's subjects. You shall also make no noise in
    the streets; for, for the watch to babble and to talk is
    most tolerable, and not to be endured.

35 1. WATCH   We will rather sleep than talk. We know what
    belongs to a watch.

DOGBERRY   Why, you speak like an ancient and most qui-
    et watchman, for I cannot see how sleeping should
    offend. Only have a care that your bills be not stolen.

40   Well, you are to call at all the alehouses and bid those
    that are drunk get them to bed.

2. WATCH   How if they will not?

DOGBERRY   Why then, let them alone till they are sober.
    If they make you not then the better answer, you may

13 **well-favored**：handsome.

17 **for your favor**：as for your appearance.

19 **no need of such vanity**：Dogberry 本应该说 need of such ability.

20 **senseless**：被 Dogberry 当作 sensible.

22—23 **lanthorn**：lantern. **comprehend**：被 Dogberry 当作 apprehend (i. e., arrest). **vagrom**：vagrant，流浪的。 **stand**：halt.

23—24 **in the Prince's name**：用王爷的名义（进行逮捕时的用语）。

25 **'a**：he.

31 **meddle with**：应为 deal with.

34 **tolerable**：被 Dogberry 当作 intolerable.

36 **belongs to**：is the duty of.

37 **ancient**：experienced.

39 **bills**：halberds，戟钺（一种两用的武器）。

41 **them**：themselves.

45   say they are not the men you took them for.

2. WATCH Well, sir.

DOGBERRY If you meet a thief, you may suspect him, by
virtue of your office, to be no true man; and for such
kind of men, the less you meddle or make with them,
50   why, the more is for your honesty.

2. WATCH If we know him to be a thief, shall we not lay
hands on him?

DOGBERRY Truly, by your office you may; but I think
they that touch pitch will be defiled. The most peace-
able way for you, if you do take a thief, is to let him
55   show himself what he is, and steal out of your company.

VERGES You have been always called a merciful man,
partner.

DOGBERRY Truly, I would not hang a dog by my will,
much more a man who hath any honesty in him.

60   VERGES If you hear a child cry in the night, you must
call to the nurse and bid her still it.

2. WATCH How if the nurse be asleep and will not hear
us?

DOGBERRY Why then, depart in peace and let the child
65   wake her with crying; for the ewe that will not hear
her lamb when it baes will never answer a calf when he
bleats.

VERGES 'Tis very true.

DOGBERRY This is the end of the charge: you, Constable, are to present the Prince's own person. If you
70   meet the Prince in the night, you may stay him.

VERGES Nay, by'r lady, that I think 'a cannot.

DOGBERRY Five shillings to one on't with any man
that knows the statutes, he may stay him! Marry, not
without the Prince be willing; for indeed the watch
75   ought to offend no man, and it is an offense to stay a

48 **true**：honest.

49 **meddle or make**：associate.

53 **they that touch pitch will be defiled**：见《圣经·外书·教士篇》第 13 章 1 节,近墨者黑。

55 **steal**：move stealthily, slip.

66 **baes**：baaes,小羊叫。 **bleats**：小牛或小羊叫。

69 **present**：被 Dogberry 当作 represent.

70 **stay**：stop.

71 **by'r lady**：by our lady（温和的赌咒语,our Lady 指圣母马丽亚）。 **that … cannot**：I think he cannot do that.

72 **Five … on't**：I'll bet five shillings to one on it. 我愿以五先令对一先令在这件事（即下面所说的 he may stay him）上打赌。

73 **statutes**：议会通过的成文法（但这种事情应属于 common law 习惯用法,Dogberry 又弄错了）。

74 **without**：unless.

75 **offense**：(in the legal sense) 过失。

man against his will.

VERGES By'r lady, I think it be so.

DOGBERRY Ha, ah, ha! Well, masters, good night. An
there be any matter of weight chances, call up me.
80   Keep your fellows' counsels and your own, and good
night. Come, neighbor.

2. WATCH Well, masters, we hear our charge. Let us go sit
here upon the church bench till two, and then all to bed.

DOGBERRY One word more, honest neighbors. I pray you
85   watch about Signior Leonato's door, for the wedding
being there to-morrow, there is a great coil to-night.
Adieu. Be vigitant, I beseech you.

> *Exeunt* [*Dogberry and Verges*].
> *Enter Borachio and Conrade.*

BORACHIO What, Conrade!

2. WATCH [*aside*] Peace! stir not!

90   BORACHIO Conrade, I say!

CONRADE Here, man. I am at thy elbow.

BORACHIO Mass, and my elbow itched! I thought there
would a scab follow.

CONRADE I will owe thee an answer for that; and now
95   forward with thy tale.

BORACHIO Stand thee close then under this penthouse,
for it drizzles rain, and I will, like a true drunkard, utter all to thee.

2. WATCH [*aside*]Some treason, masters. Yet stand close.

BORACHIO Therefore know I have earned of Don John a
100   thousand ducats.

CONRADE Is it possible that any villainy should be so
dear?

BORACHIO Thou shouldst rather ask if it were possible
any villainy should be so rich; for when rich villains
105   have need of poor ones, poor ones may make what
price they will.

78 **Ha, ah, ha!**: a pompous clearing of the throat, and not laughter. **masters**: 伙计们。 **An**: if.

79 **matter of weight**: important thing. **chances**: which happens. **call up me**: call me up.

80 **Keep ··· counsels**: keep secret what you know.

83 **church bench**: 教堂门廊里的石凳。

86 **coil**: bustle.

87 **vigitant**: 被 Dogberry 当作 vigilant.

92 **Mass**: 为 by the Mass 的简略说法，表感叹。

93 **scab**: 双关语 1. 疥癣；2. 恶棍。

94 **owe thee an answer**: answer that later.

95 **forward with thy tale**: tell your story.

96 **penthouse**: open shed with a sloping roof.

97 **drunkard**: 他的名字源于西班牙文 boracho，意思是 drunkard. （英谚）The drunkard tells all.

98 **stand close**: keep quiet and out of sight.

99 **of**: from.

102 **dear**: expensive.

104 **be so rich**: can afford to pay so much.

105 **make**: ask.

CONRADE   I wonder at it.

BORACHIO   That shows thou art unconfirmed. Thou know-
est that the fashion of a doublet, or a hat, or a cloak,
110   is nothing to a man.

CONRADE   Yes, it is apparel.

BORACHIO   I mean the fashion.

CONRADE   Yes, the fashion is the fashion.

BORACHIO   Tush! I may as well say the fool's the fool.
115   But seest thou not what a deformed thief this fashion is?

1. WATCH   [*aside*] I know that Deformed. 'A has been a
vile thief this seven year; 'a goes up and down like a
gentleman. I remember his name.

BORACHIO   Didst thou not hear somebody?

120   CONRADE   No; 'twas the vane on the house.

BORACHIO   Seest thou not, I say, what a deformed thief
this fashion is? how giddily 'a turns about all the
hot-bloods between fourteen and five-and-thirty?
sometimes fashioning them like Pharaoh's soldiers in
125   the reechy painting, sometime like god Bel's priests in
the old church window, sometime like the shaven Hercules in the smirched worm-eaten tapestry, where his
codpiece seems as massy as his club?

CONRADE   All this I see; and I see that the fashion wears
130   out more apparel than the man. But art not thou thy-
self giddy with the fashion too, that thou hast shifted
out of thy tale into telling me of the fashion?

BORACHIO   Not so neither. But know that I have tonight
wooed Margaret, the Lady Hero's gentlewoman, by
135   the name of Hero. She leans me out at her mistress'
chamber window, bids me a thousand times good night
— I tell this tale vilely; I should first tell thee how the
Prince, Claudio, and my master, planted and placed
and possessed by my master Don John, saw afar off in
140   the orchard this amiable encounter.

108 **unconfirmed**：inexperienced.

110 **is nothing to a man**：双关语 1. tells us nothing about a man；
2. is of no consequence to a man.

114 **Tush!**：表示不满与责备的感叹词。

115 **deformed thief**：deforming rascal.

116 **Deformed**：畸形儿(指 Borachio).   **'A**：he.

117 **goes up and down**：walks about.

120 **vane**：weather vane, 风向标。

123 **hot-bloods**：fiery-spirited young men.

124 **Pharaoh** [ˈfɛərəu]：法老(古埃及国王)。

125 **reechy**：dirty.   **Bel**：Baal(犹太迦南地区的土地神),见《圣
经•外书•贝尔和龙》。

128 **codpiece**：front part of breeches，often stuffed and ornamen-
ted.   **massy**：large.

129—130 **fashion … man**：由于式样改变而丢弃的衣服多于穿
旧、穿破的衣服。

133 **Not so neither**：not so either.

135 **leans me out**："me" is here emphatic，drawing attention to
the speaker，and is equivalent to "mark me", "I tell you".

137 **vilely**：badly.

139 **possessed**：instructed. planted，placed and possessed 三字押
头韵。

140 **amiable encounter**：lovers' meeting.

CONRADE   And thought they Margaret was Hero?

BORACHIO   Two of them did, the Prince and Claudio;
but the devil my master knew she was Margaret; and
partly by his oaths, which first possessed them, partly
145   by the dark night, which did deceive them, but chiefly
by my villainy, which did confirm any slander that Don
John had made, away went Claudio enraged; swore he
would meet her, as he was appointed, next morning at
the temple, and there, before the whole congregation,
150   shame her with what he saw o'ernight and send her
home again without a husband.

1. WATCH   We charge you in the Prince's name stand!

2. WATCH   Call up the right master constable. We have
here recovered the most dangerous piece of lechery that
155   ever was known in the commonwealth.

1. WATCH   And one Deformed is one of them. I know
him; 'a wears a lock.

CONRADE   Masters, masters —

2. WATCH   You'll be made bring Deformed forth, I war-
160   rant you.

CONRADE   Masters —

2. WATCH   Never speak, we charge you. Let us obey you
to go with us.

BORACHIO   We are like to prove a goodly commodity,
165   being taken up of these men's bills.

CONRADE   A commodity in question, I warrant you.
Come, we'll obey you.   *Exeunt*.

SCENE IV

The house of Leonato

Enter Hero, and Margaret and Ursula.

HERO   Good Ursula, wake my cousin Beatrice and desire

144　**possessed**：took possession of，dominated.

149　**temple**：church.

153　**the right**：一种尊称。

154　**recovered**：the second watchman's mistake for 'discovered'. **lechery**：his mistake for 'treachery'.

155　**commonwealth**：国家。

157　**lock**：lovelock，hanging curl which was fashionable among some men of the age.

159　**made bring**：made to bring.

162　**obey**：a mistake for 'order'.

164　**like**：likely.　**a goodly commodity**：双关语 1. 一批好货；2. 一笔好生意。

165　**taken up**：双关语 1. 逮捕；2. 借来。　**of**：双关语 1. on the strength of；2. in exchange for.　**bills**：双关语 1. 戟；2. 货单。

166　**in question**：双关语 1. 待受审问；2. 价值可疑。

her to rise.

URSULA I will, lady.

HERO And bid her come hither.

5 URSULA Well.   [*Exit.*]

MARGARET Troth, I think your other rebato were better.

HERO No, pray thee, good Meg, I'll wear this.

MARGARET By my troth, 's not so good, and I warrant
your cousin will say so.

10 HERO My cousin's a fool, and thou art another. I'll
wear none but this.

MARGARET I like the new tire within excellently, if the
hair were a thought browner; and your gown's a most
rare fashion, i' faith. I saw the Duchess of Milan's

15 gown that they praise so.

HERO O, that exceeds, they say.

MARGARET By my troth, 's but a nightgown in respect
of yours — cloth a gold and cuts, and laced with silver, set with pearls, down sleeves, side-sleeves, and

20 skirts, round underborne with a bluish tinsel. But for a
fine, quaint, graceful, and excellent fashion, yours is
worth ten on 't.

HERO God give me joy to wear it! for my heart is exceeding heavy.

MARGARET 'Twill be heavier soon by the weight of a man.

25 HERO Fie upon thee! art not ashamed?

MARGARET Of what, lady? of speaking honorably? Is not
marriage honorable in a beggar? Is not your lord honorable without marriage? I think you would have me say,
'saving your reverence, a husband.' An bad thinking

30 do not wrest true speaking. I'll offend nobody. Is
there any harm in 'the heavier for a husband'? None, I
think, an it be the right husband and the right wife.
Otherwise 'tis light, and not heavy. Ask my Lady Beatrice else. Here she comes.

III. iv

6 **rebato**：宽而硬的轮状皱领。   **were**：虚拟语气，表委婉。

7 **Meg**：Margaret 的爱称。

12 **tire**：head-dress，头巾，头饰。   **within**：in the room within, not seen on the stage.

13—14 **a thought**：a little.   **a most rare fashion**：of a most rare fashion.

16 **exceeds**：is most superior.

17—18 **'s**：it's.   **nightgown**：dressing-gown.   **in respect of**：in comparison with.

18—19 **cloth a gold**：cloth of gold，金线织的缎子。   **cuts**：slashes to show the underbody，镂空的花样。   **laced with silver**：镶着银色花边。

19 **down sleeves**：full-length sleeves.   **side-sleeves**：ornamental open sleeves hanging from the shoulder.

20 **skirts，round underborne with a bluish tinsel**：圆形的裙子，下面用蓝色金属箔将它撑起。

21 **quaint**：elegant.

22 **on 't**：of it.

27 **in**：even in.

29 **saving your reverence**：without offense to you，相当于 beg your pardon.   **An**：if.   **bad**：malicious，恶意的。

30 **wrest**：twist.

33—34 **light**：双关语 1. 轻；2. 放荡。   **else**：if it be otherwise.

Enter Beatrice.

35 HERO Good morrow, coz.

BEATRICE Good morrow, sweet Hero.

HERO Why, how now? Do you speak in the sick tune?

BEATRICE I am out of all other tune, methinks.

MARGARET Clap's into 'Light a love. ' That goes with-

40   out a burden. Do you sing it, and I'll dance it.

BEATRICE Ye light a love with your heels! then, if your
husband have stables enough, you'll see he shall lack
no barnes.

MARGARET O illegitimate construction! I scorn that with

45   my heels.

BEATRICE 'Tis almost five o'clock, cousin; 'tis time you
were ready. By my troth, I am exceeding ill. Hey-ho!

MARGARET For a hawk, a horse, or a husband?

BEATRICE For the letter that begins them all, H.

50 MARGARET Well, an you be not turned Turk, there's no
more sailing by the star.

BEATRICE What means the fool, trow?

MARGARET Nothing I; but God send every one their
heart's desire!

55 HERO These gloves the Count sent me, they are an excellent perfume.

BEATRICE I am stuffed, cousin; I cannot smell.

MARGARET A maid, and stuffed! There's goodly catch-
ing of cold.

60 BEATRICE O, God help me! God help me! How long
have you professed apprehension?

MARGARET Ever since you left it. Doth not my wit become me rarely?

BEATRICE It is not seen enough. You should wear it in

65   your cap. By my troth, I am sick.

MARGARET Get you some of this distilled *carduus benedictus* and lay it to your heart. It is the only thing for a

35　**Good morrow**：good morning.　**coz**：cousin.

37　**how now?**：What is the meaning of this?　**tune**：mood.

39　**Clap's into**：clap us into，i. e.，let us begin briskly.　**'Light a love'**：'Light of love'为古老曲调名。

40　**burden**：双关语 1. refrain 叠句；2. 负担，与 heavier for a husband 意思相关。

41　**Ye light a love with your heels!**：You be light of love（wanton）with your heels（in dancing）. light-heeled 又解 unchaste.

43　**barnes**：双关语 1. barns 粮草棚，牛棚；2. bairns 小孩。

44—45　**illegitimate construction!**：illogical interpretation.　**I ... heels**：I kick that away scornfully.

47　**Hey-ho!**：这里是表示烦闷，但又可用于对猎鹰或马的呼喊。

49　**H**：H 与当时 ache 的发音都是［eitʃ］，因此构成双关语。

50　**an**：if.　**turned Turk**：turned pagan，completely changed. 这里是说 Beatrice 变了。

51　**star**：North star.

52　**trow**：I wonder.

53　**God send ...**：May God send ...，见《圣经·旧约·诗篇》第 39 章 4 节。

55　**are**：have.

57　**stuffed**：nose stopped with a cold.

58　**stuffed**：copulated with.　**goodly**：nice(反语)。

61　**professed apprehension**：claimed to have sharp wit，自以为聪明。

62—63　**it**：指 apprehension，wit.　**become**：suit.　**rarely**：excellently.

64—65　**wear ... cap**：like a feather for an ostentatious ornament.

66—67　*carduus benedictus*〈拉丁语〉：blessed thistle 被认为是一种万灵药。benedictus 与 Benedick 谐音。

qualm.

HERO   There thou prick'st her with a thistle.

70   BEATRICE   Benedictus! why Benedictus? You have some
moral in this Benedictus.

MARGARET   Moral? No, by my troth, I have no moral
meaning; I meant plain holy thistle. You may think perchance that I think you are in love. Nay, by'r lady, I

75   am not such a fool to think what I list; nor I list not to
think what I can; nor indeed I cannot think, if I would
think my heart out of thinking, that you are in love,
or that you will be in love, or that you can be in love.
Yet Benedick was such another, and now is he become a

80   man. He swore he would never marry, and yet now in
.   despite of his heart he eats his meat without grudging;
and how you may be converted I know not, but methinks you look with your eyes as other women do.

BEATRICE   What pace is this that thy tongue keeps?

85   MARGARET   Not a false gallop.

Enter Ursula.

URSULA   Madam, withdraw. The Prince, the Count, Signior Benedick, Don John, and all the gallants of the
town are come to fetch you to church.

HERO   Help to dress me, good coz, good Meg, good Ur-
sula.   [*Exeunt.*]

SCENE V

The house of Leonato

Enter Leonato and the Constable [*Dogberry*]
and the Headborough [*Verges*].

LEONATO   What would you with me, honest neighbor?

DOGBERRY   Marry, sir, I would have some confidence
with you that decerns you nearly.

LEONATO   Brief, I pray you, for you see it is a busy time

68   **qualm**: sudden sickness.

71   **moral**: hidden meaning,寓意。

73—74   **perchance**: perhaps.

75   **list**: like, please.

79—80   **become a man**: become a normal man.

81   **eats** ⋯ **grudging**: has a normal appetite.

85   **Not** ⋯ **gallop**: properly a canter, but Margaret quibbles, meaning 'I speak truth.'

III. v

1   **What** ⋯ **me**: What is your wish with me.

2   **confidence**: a mistake for 'conference'.

3   **decerns**: a mistake for 'concerns'.   **nearly**: closely.

5   with me.

DOGBERRY Marry, this it is, sir.

VERGES Yes, in truth it is, sir.

LEONATO What is it, my good friends?

DOGBERRY Goodman Verges, sir, speaks a little off the
10   matter — an old man, sir, and his wits are not so blunt
       as, God help, I would desire they were; but, in faith,
       honest at the skin between his brows.

VERGES Yes, I thank God I am as honest as any man liv-
       ing that is an old man and no honester than I.

15 DOGBERRY Comparisons are odorous. Palabras, neighbor
       Verges.

LEONATO Neighbors, you are tedious.

DOGBERRY It pleases your worship to say so, but we are
       the poor Duke's officers; but truly, for mine own part,
20   if I were as tedious as a king, I could find in my heart
       to bestow it all of your worship.

LEONATO All thy tediousness on me, ah?

DOGBERRY Yea, an 'twere a thousand pound more than
       'tis; for I hear as good exclamation on your worship
25   as of any man in the city, and though I be but a poor
       man, I am glad to hear it.

VERGES And so am I.

LEONATO I would fain know what you have to say.

VERGES Marry, sir, our watch to-night, excepting your
30   worship's presence, ha' ta'en a couple of as arrant
       knaves as any in Messina.

DOGBERRY A good old man, sir; he will be talking. As
       they say, 'When the age is in, the wit is out.' God
       help us! it is a world to see! Well said, i' faith, neigh-
35   bor Verges. Well, God's a good man. An two men
       ride of a horse, one must ride behind. An honest soul,
       i' faith, sir, by my troth he is, as ever broke bread;
       but God is to be worshipped; all men are not alike,

9—10　Goodman：用于名字之前作称呼。　　**off the matter**：off the point.　**blunt**：a mistake for 'sharp'.

12　honest … brows：a common proverb，perhaps explained by another，'Everyone's fault is written in his forehead.'源于过去在罪犯额头加盖烙印,因此额上无烙印可作为诚实的证明。

15　odorous：a mistake for 'odious'.　**Palabras**：from Spanish pocas palabras ＝ few words，be brief — a common phrase of the time.

19　poor Duke's：a mistake for 'Duke's poor'.

20　as tedious as a king：Dogberry mistakes 'tedious' for a good word.

21　of：on.

24　exclamation：a mistake for 'acclamation'（欢呼）。

29　to-night：last night.　**excepting**：a mistake for 'respecting'. respecting your presence 为表示尊敬的套语。

30—31　as arrant knaves as：knaves as arrant（errant，wandering，转意 downright）as.

32　he … talking：will 重读,表示坚持某一动作(他硬是要一直讲下去)。

33　'When … out'：(谚语) When ale is in, wit is out 的讹变。

34　it is a world：it is a marvel (a proverbial phrase).

35—36　God's a good man：a proverbial phrase，meaning 'God is good!'　**An**：if.　**ride of**：ride on.

alas, good neighbor!

LEONATO Indeed, neighbor, he comes too short of you.

40 DOGBERRY Gifts that God gives.

LEONATO I must leave you.

DOGBERRY One word, sir. Our watch, sir, have indeed comprehended two aspicious persons, and we would have them this morning examined before your worship.

45 LEONATO Take their examination yourself and bring it me. I am now in great haste, as it may appear unto you.

DOGBERRY It shall be suffigance.

LEONATO Drink some wine ere you go. Fare you well.

[Enter a Messenger.]

MESSENGER My lord, they stay for you to give your
50 daughter to her husband.

LEONATO I'll wait upon them. I am ready.

Exeunt Leonato and Messenger.

DOGBERRY Go, good partner, go get you to Francis Seacole. Bid him bring his pen and inkhorn to the jail. We are now to examination these men.

55 VERGES And we must do it wisely.

DOGBERRY We will spare for no wit, I warrant you. Here's that shall drive some of them to a non-come. Only get the learned writer to set down our excommunication, and meet me at the jail. *[Exeunt.]*

39   he comes too short of you：他远不及你(个子大，饶舌)。

40   Gifts that God gives：Mine are gifts that God gives me.

43   comprehended：a mistake for 'apprehended'.   **aspicious**：a mistake for 'suspicious'.

47   suffigance：a mistake for 'sufficient'.

49   stay for：are waiting for（当时常以一般现在时代替现在进行时）。

51   I'll … them：我就去他们那里。

54   examination：a mistake for 'examine'.

56   spare for：spare.

57   that：what.   **non-come**：perhaps Dogberry means 'nonplus'（迷惑，为难）。

58—59   excommunication：a mistake for 'examination'.

ACT IV

SCENE I

Within a Church in Messina

Enter Prince [Don Pedro], [John the]
Bastard, Leonato, Friar [Francis],
Claudio, Benedick, Hero, and Beatrice
[and Attendants].

LEONATO   Come, Friar Francis, be brief. Only to the
plain form of marriage, and you shall recount their particular duties afterwards.

FRIAR   You come hither, my lord, to marry this lady?

5   CLAUDIO   No.

LEONATO   To be married to her. Friar, you come to marry her.

FRIAR   Lady, you come hither to be married to this
count?

HERO   I do.

10   FRIAR   If either of you know any inward impediment why
you should not be conjoined, I charge you on your
souls to utter it.

CLAUDIO   Know you any, Hero?

HERO   None, my lord.

15   FRIAR   Know you any, Count?

LEONATO   I dare make his answer — none.

CLAUDIO   O, what men dare do! what men may do! what
men daily do, not knowing what they do!

BENEDICK   How now? interjections? Why then, some be

20   of laughing, as, ah, ha, he!

CLAUDIO

IV. i

2   plain form: simple prescribed formula, with the preamble in the service on the responsibilities of marriage omitted.

10   inward: secret.

11—12   conjoined: joined, united.   **on your souls**: 以你们的灵魂作担保。

19—20   some … , he!: Benedick 听到 Claudio 用一连串惊叹语，就开玩笑地引用 Lily 的拉丁语法中关于感叹词的话 'Some are of laughing: as, ah, ha, he!'.

Stand thee by, friar. Father, by your leave,
Will you with free and unconstrainèd soul
Give me this maid your daughter?

LEONATO

As freely, son, as God did give her me.

CLAUDIO

25 And what have I to give you back whose worth
May counterpoise this rich and precious gift?

PEDRO

Nothing, unless you render her again.

CLAUDIO

Sweet Prince, you learn me noble thankfulness.
There, Leonato, take her back again.
30 Give not this rotten orange to your friend.
She's but the sign and semblance of her honor.
Behold how like a maid she blushes here!
O, what authority and show of truth
Can cunning sin cover itself withal!
35 Comes not that blood as modest evidence
To witness simple virtue? Would you not swear,
All you that see her, that she were a maid,
By these exterior shows? But she is none:
She knows the heat of a luxurious bed;
40 Her blush is guiltiness, not modesty.

LEONATO

What do you mean, my lord?

CLAUDIO   Not to be married,
Not to knit my soul to an approvèd wanton.

LEONATO

Dear my lord, if you, in your own proof,
Have vanquished the resistance of her youth
45 And made defeat of her virginity —

CLAUDIO

I know what you would say. If I have known her,

21 **Stand thee by**：stand aside(命令句中 thou 改为 thee)． **by your leave**：if you permit me to call you so.

25 **whose worth**：the worth of which（whose 的先行词为 what).

26 **counterpoise**：offset，compensate.

27 **render her again**：give her back.

28 **Sweet**：dear． **learn**：teach.

31 **She's … honor**：She only looks honest． **but**：merely.

33 **authority**：assurance，自信。

34 **withal**：with(此句的主语为 sin).

35 **blood as modest evidence**：blush as evidence of modesty.

36 **witness**：bear witness to.

37 **were**：虚拟语气，表示与事实不符。

39 **heat**：passion． **luxurious**：lustful. luxurious 与 bed 连用，系移位修饰语。

42 **approvèd**：proved． **wanton**：荡妇。

43 **in your own proof**：in your own attempt to test her． **proof**：trial，test.

45 **made defeat of**：defeated (made her lose).

46 **have known**：had sexual intercourse with.

You will say she did embrace me as a husband,
And so extenuate the forehand sin.
No, Leonato,

50   I never tempted her with word too large,
But, as a brother to his sister, showed
Bashful sincerity and comely love.

HERO

And seemed I ever otherwise to you?

CLAUDIO

Out on thee seeming! I will write against it.

55   You seem to me as Dian in her orb,
As chaste as is the bud ere it be blown;
But you are more intemperate in your blood
Than Venus, or those pamp'red animals
That rage in savage sensuality.

HERO

60   Is my lord well that he doth speak so wide?

LEONATO

Sweet Prince, why speak not you?

PEDRO   What should I speak?
I stand dishonored that have gone about
To link my dear friend to a common stale.

LEONATO

Are these things spoken, or do I but dream?

JOHN

65   Sir, they are spoken, and these things are true.

BENEDICK

This looks not like a nuptial.

HERO   'True'! O God!

CLAUDIO

Leonato, stand I here?
Is this the Prince? Is this the Prince's brother?
Is this face Hero's? Are our eyes our own?

LEONATO

48 **forehand**：beforehand，premarriage.

50 **large**：free, immodest.

52 **comely**：decent.

54 **Out on**：shame on.　**seeming**：包括 appearing 和 pretending 两种意义。　**write against**：denounce.

55 **Dian**：Diana 罗马神话中的月亮女神，也是贞洁女神。　**orb**：sphere, the moon.

56 **ere**：before.　**be blown**：be fully opened.

57 **intemperate**：ungoverned.　**blood**：sensual appetite.

58 **Venus**：罗马神话中的爱情女神。　**pamp'red**：fed to the full.

59 **rage**：behave wantonly.

60 **wide**：far from the truth.

62 **stand**：be in specified situation.　**gone about**：undertaken.

63 **common**：base, low.　**stale**：prostitute.

70 All this is so; but what of this, my lord?

CLAUDIO

 Let me but move one question to your daughter,
 And by that fatherly and kindly power
 That you have in her, bid her answer truly.

LEONATO

 I charge thee do so, as thou art my child.

HERO

75 O, God defend me! How am I beset!
 What kind of catechising call you this?

CLAUDIO

 To make you answer truly to your name.

HERO

 Is it not Hero? Who can blot that name
 With any just reproach?

CLAUDIO   Marry, that can Hero!

80 Hero itself can blot out Hero's virtue.
 What man was he talked with you yesternight,
 Out at your window betwixt twelve and one?
 Now, if you are a maid, answer to this.

HERO

 I talked with no man at that hour, my lord.

PEDRO

85 Why, then are you no maiden. Leonato,
 I am sorry you must hear. Upon mine honor
 Myself, my brother, and this grievèd Count
 Did see her, hear her, at that hour last night
 Talk with a ruffian at her chamber window,

90 Who hath indeed, most like a liberal villain,
 Confessed the vile encounters they have had
 A thousand times in secret.

JOHN

 Fie, fie! they are not to be named, my lord —
 Not to be spoke of;

71 **move**：put.

72 **by**：凭。 **kindly**：natural.

73 **truly**：truthfully, honestly.

76 **catechising**：教义问答（意即严格的诘问）。

77 **To … name**：教义问答的第一个问题是"What is your name?" Claudio 有意地问 Hero 是否与自己的名字相称。按古希腊故事中，Hero 是 Leander 的忠贞的爱人。

80 **Hero itself**：the name Hero (by which he had heard Borachio call Margaret).

81 **he talked**：he who talked.

83 **answer to**：explain.

87 **grievèd**：wronged, deceived.

90 **liberal**：libertine, licentious.

94 **spoke**：spoken.

95   There is not chastity enough in language
        Without offense to utter them. Thus, pretty lady,
        I am sorry for thy much misgovernment.

CLAUDIO

        O Hero! what a Hero hadst thou been
        If half thy outward graces had been placed
100   About thy thoughts and counsels of thy heart!
        But fare thee well, most foul, most fair! Farewell,
        Thou pure impiety and impious purity!
        For thee I'll lock up all the gates of love,
        And on my eyelids shall conjecture hang,
105   To turn all beauty into thoughts of harm,
        And never shall it more be gracious.

LEONATO

        Hath no man's dagger here a point for me?
            [*Hero swoons.*]

BEATRICE

        Why, how now, cousin? Wherefore sink you down?

JOHN

        Come let us go. These things, come thus to light,
110   Smother her spirits up.

                    Exeunt Don Pedro, Don John, and Claudio.

BENEDICK

        How doth the lady?

BEATRICE   Dead, I think. Help, uncle!
        Hero! why Hero! Uncle! Signior Benedick! Friar!

LEONATO

        O Fate, take not away thy heavy hand!
        Death is the fairest cover for her shame
115   That may be wished for.

BEATRICE   How now, cousin Hero?

FRIAR   Have comfort, lady.

LEONATO   Dost thou look up?

FRIAR   Yea, wherefore should she not?

95—96   **There ··· them**：there is not enough chastity in language for us to describe the encounters without giving offense.

97   **much misgovernment**：grave misconduct.

99—100   **outward graces**：good qualities in appearance.   **placed about**：transferred to.

102   **Thou ··· purity!**：这句话使用矛盾修饰语（oxymoron），再加上互换的重复表示强调。

104—105   **conjecture**：doubt，suspicion.   **And ··· harm**：Hereafter whenever I see any beautiful woman I shall suspect her，thinking she will do harm to me.

106   **more be gracious**：be finding favor any more.

107   **point**：sharp end.

110   **spirits**：vital powers，consciousness.

LEONATO

    Wherefore? Why, doth not every earthly thing

    Cry shame upon her? Could she here deny

120   The story that is printed in her blood?

    Do not live, Hero; do not ope thine eyes;

    For, did I think thou wouldst not quickly die,

    Thought I thy spirits were stronger than thy shames,

    Myself would on the rearward of reproaches

125   Strike at thy life. Grieved I, I had but one?

    Chid I for that at frugal nature's frame?

    O, one too much by thee! Why had I one?

    Why ever wast thou lovely in my eyes?

    Why had I not with charitable hand

130   Took up a beggar's issue at my gates,

    Who smirchèd thus and mired with infamy,

    I might have said, 'No part of it is mine;

    This shame derives itself from unknown loins'?

    But mine, and mine I loved, and mine I praised,

135   And mine that I was proud on — mine so much

    That I myself was to myself not mine,

    Valuing of her — why she. O, she is fall'n

    Into a pit of ink, that the wide sea

    Hath drops too few to wash her clean again,

140   And salt too little which may season give

    To her foul tainted flesh!

BENEDICK Sir, sir, be patient. For my part, I am so at-

    tired in wonder, I know not what to say.

BEATRICE

    O, on my soul, my cousin is belied!

BENEDICK

145   Lady, were you her bedfellow last night?

BEATRICE

    No, truly, not; although, until last night,

    I have this twelvemonth been her bedfellow.

118 earthly：用于加强 thing 的语气。

120 printed in her blood?：written in her blushes.

121 ope：open.

122—125 For 以下一句，可意译如下：If I think that you would not quickly die，that your vitality would prove stronger than your shame，I myself would kill you immediately after reproaching you.

124 on the rearward of：immediately after.

125 Grieved … one?：Did I feel sorry that I had only one child? 用过去时是表示他认为 Hero 等于已死。

126 Chid … frame?：Did I blame that fact on the design of niggardly Nature?

127 much：many.   **by thee!**：表比较差别之量。

130 issue：child.

131 Who … infamy：为独立主格结构。

133 loins：parents(为提喻 synecdoche)。

134 mine：my issue.

135 proud on：proud of.

136—137 That … her：that in caring so much for her，I had no regard for myself.

138 that：so that.

140 give：provide a preservative (seasoning) to keep fresh,起防腐作用。

142—143 attired：wrapped up.

144 is belied：has had lies told about her, is falsely accused.

LEONATO

    Confirmed, confirmed! O, that is stronger made

    Which was before barred up with ribs of iron!

150   Would the two princes lie? and Claudio lie,

    Who loved her so that, speaking of her foulness,

    Washed it with tears? Hence from her! let her die.

FRIAR

    Hear me a little;

    For I have only been silent so long,

155   And given way unto this course of fortune,

    By noting of the lady. I have marked

    A thousand blushing apparitions

    To start into her face, a thousand innocent shames

    In angel whiteness beat away those blushes,

160   And in her eye there hath appeared a fire

    To burn the errors that these princes hold

    Against her maiden truth. Call me a fool;

    Trust not my reading nor my observations,

    Which with experimental seal doth warrant

165   The tenure of my book; trust not my age,

    My reverence, calling, nor divinity,

    If this sweet lady lie not guiltless here

    Under some biting error.

LEONATO   Friar, it cannot be.

    Thou seest that all the grace that she hath left

170   Is that she will not add to her damnation

    A sin of perjury: she not denies it.

    Why seek'st thou then to cover with excuse

    That which appears in proper nakedness?

FRIAR

    Lady, what man is he you are accused of?

HERO

175   They know that do accuse me; I know none.

    If I know more of any man alive

148   **stronger made**: reinforced.

151   **so that**: so much that.

155   **given ... fortune**: allowed the course of events to go on.

156   **By noting of**: because I have been carefully watching.

157   **blushing apparitions**: blushes (personified).

159   **angel whiteness**: angelic paleness.

164   **experimental seal**: seal of experience.   **warrant**: confirm.

165   **tenure of my book**: tenor (substance) of my reading (interpretation of her expression).

169   **grace**: sense of propriety.   **that ... left**: that is left in her possession.

171   **not denies**: does not deny.

173   **proper**: true.

175   **They ... me**: They who accuse me know.

Than that which maiden modesty doth warrant,
Let all my sins lack mercy! O my father,
Prove you that any man with me conversed
180   At hours unmeet, or that I yesternight
Maintained the change of words with any creature,
Refuse me, hate me, torture me to death!

FRIAR

There is some strange misprision in the princes.

BENEDICK

Two of them have the very bent of honor;
185   And if their wisdoms be misled in this,
The practice of it lives in John the bastard,
Whose spirits toil in frame of villainies.

LEONATO

I know not. If they speak but truth of her,
These hands shall tear her. If they wrong her honor,
190   The proudest of them shall well hear of it.
Time hath not yet so dried this blood of mine,
Nor age so eat up my invention,
Nor fortune made such havoc of my means,
Nor my bad life reft me so much of friends,
195   But they shall find awaked in such a kind
Both strength of limb and policy of mind,
Ability in means, and choice of friends,
To quit me of them throughly.

FRIAR   Pause awhile

And let my counsel sway you in this case.
200   Your daughter here the princes (left for dead),
Let her awhile be secretly kept in,
And publish it that she is dead indeed;
Maintain a mourning ostentation,
And on your family's old monument
205   Hang mournful epitaphs, and do all rites
That appertain unto a burial.

178 **sins lack mercy!**：按基督教义：人人有罪，靠上帝的恩典才能得救；没有神恩，则沉沦下地狱。

180 **unmeet**：improper.

181 **Maintained**：carried on. **change**：exchange.

182 **Refuse**：disown.

183 **misprision**：mistake, misunderstanding.

184 **very bent of**：highest degree of.

186 **practice**：plotting, treacherous contriving.

187 **in frame of**：in framing.

190 **shall well hear of it**：shall be severely reprimanded.

192 **eat**：eaten. **invention**：inventiveness, power to make plans.

193 **means**：resources.

194 **reft**：bereft, deprived.

195 **But**：that … not（与前面的 not 连用，两个否定强调的一个肯定）。 **kind**：manner.

196 **policy of mind**：mental prudence.

197 **choice of friends**：many good friends.

198 **quit … throughly**：settle accounts thoroughly with them.

201 **in**：at home.

203 **Maintain … ostentation**：perform the formal show of mourning.

LEONATO

What shall become of this? What will this do?

FRIAR

Marry, this well carried shall on her behalf

Change slander to remorse. That is some good.

210   But not for that dream I on this strange course,

But on this travail look for greater birth.

She dying, as it must be so maintained,

Upon the instant that she was accused,

Shall be lamented, pitied, and excused

215   Of every hearer; for it so falls out

That what we have we prize not to the worth

Whiles we enjoy it, but being lacked and lost,

Why, then we rack the value, then we find

The virtue that possession would not show us

220   Whiles it was ours. So will it fare with Claudio.

When he shall hear she died upon his words,

Th' idea of her life shall sweetly creep

Into his study of imagination,

And every lovely organ of her life

225   Shall come apparelled in more precious habit,

More moving, delicate, and full of life,

Into the eye and prospect of his soul

Than when she lived indeed. Then shall he mourn

(If ever love had interest in his liver)

230   And wish he had not so accusèd her —

No, though he thought his accusation true.

Let this be so, and doubt not but success

Will fashion the event in better shape

Than I can lay it down in likelihood.

235   But if all aim but this be levelled false,

The supposition of the lady's death

Will quench the wonder of her infamy.

And if it sort not well, you may conceal her,

208 **carried**：managed.

209 **remorse**：sorrow, grief.

210 **on**：of.

211 **on this travail**：as a result of this effort（travail 还有分娩之义）。

212 **She dying**：She having died.

213 **Upon the instant**：immediately.

215 **Of**：by. **falls out**：happens.

216 **to the worth**：for what it is worth.

218 **rack**：stretch.

220 **Whiles**：while. **fare with**：be the case with.

222 **idea … life**：memory of her.

223 **study of imagination**：imaginative study, reflection.

224 **organ of her life**：feature of her when she was alive.

225 **habit**：clothing.

226 **moving**：affecting, 动人的。

227 **prospect**：sight, view.

228 **indeed**：in fact.

229 **liver**：regarded as the seat of love.

232 **success**：what succeeds or follows.

233 **event**：outcome, result.

234 **likelihood**：supposition.

235 **be levelled false**：be directed falsely (and so miss the mark). if 从句可意译为 if we miss our aim in every other respect except this (the supposition, in the next line).

237 **quench**：suppress. **wonder of**：astonishment at.

238 **sort**：turn out.

As best befits her wounded reputation,
240   In some reclusive and religious life,
Out of all eyes, tongues, minds, and injuries.

BENEDICK
Signior Leonato, let the friar advise you;
And though you know my inwardness and love
Is very much unto the Prince and Claudio,
245   Yet, by mine honor, I will deal in this
As secretly and justly as your soul
Should with your body.

LEONATO   Being that I flow in grief,
The smallest twine may lead me.

FRIAR
'Tis well consented. Presently away;
250   For to strange sores strangely they strain the cure.
Come, lady, die to live. This wedding day
Perhaps is but prolonged. Have patience and endure.

Exit [*with all but Beatrice and Benedick*].

BENEDICK Lady Beatrice, have you wept all this while?
BEATRICE Yea, and I will weep a while longer.
255 BENEDICK I will not desire that.
BEATRICE You have no reason. I do it freely.
BENEDICK Surely I do believe your fair cousin is wronged.
BEATRICE Ah, how much might the man deserve of me
that would right her!
260 BENEDICK Is there any way to show such friendship?
BEATRICE A very even way, but no such friend.
BENEDICK May a man do it?
BEATRICE It is a man's office, but not yours.

BENEDICK I do love nothing in the world so well as you.
265   Is not that strange?

BEATRICE As strange as the thing I know not. It were as
possible for me to say I loved nothing so well as you.
But believe me not; and yet I lie not. I confess nothing,

240 **reclusive**：retired，cloistered，隐居的。

243 **inwardness**：intimacy，friendly attachment，私交。

247 **Should with**：should deal in this with. **Being that**：since. **flow**：am afloat（and hence easily pulled）．

248 **twine**：string.

249 **Presently**：immediately.

250 **to … cure**：a variant of the common proverb，'A desperate disease must have a desperate cure.' **strain**：urge，require. 这行中 to 和 they 都是多余的垫词。

251 **to**：in order to.

252 **prolonged**：postponed.

256 **freely**：of my own free will.

258—259 **deserve of me**：worthy of my reward. **that would right her**：who would avenge her wrong，为她申冤。

261 **even**：direct.

263 **office**：task.

266—267 **It … possible**：It seems as if it were possible.

nor I deny nothing. I am sorry for my cousin.

270 BENEDICK By my sword, Beatrice, thou lovest me.

BEATRICE Do not swear and eat it.

BENEDICK I will swear by it that you love me, and I will
make him eat it that says I love not you.

BEATRICE Will you not eat your word?

275 BENEDICK With no sauce that can be devised to it. I protest I love thee.

BEATRICE Why then, God forgive me!

BENEDICK What offense, sweet Beatrice?

BEATRICE You have stayed me in a happy hour. I was

280 about to protest I loved you.

BENEDICK And do it with all thy heart.

BEATRICE I love you with so much of my heart that none
is left to protest.

BENEDICK Come, bid me do anything for thee.

285 BEATRICE Kill Claudio.

BENEDICK Ha! not for the wide world!

BEATRICE You kill me to deny it. Farewell.

BENEDICK Tarry, sweet Beatrice.

BEATRICE I am gone, though I am here. There is no love

290 in you. Nay, I pray you let me go.

BENEDICK Beatrice —

BEATRICE In faith, I will go.

BENEDICK We'll be friends first.

BEATRICE You dare easier be friends with me than fight

295 with mine enemy.

BENEDICK Is Claudio thine enemy?

BEATRICE Is 'a not approved in the height a villain, that
hath slandered, scorned, dishonored my kinswoman?
O that I were a man! What? bear her in hand until they

300 come to take hands, and then with public accusation,
uncovered slander, unmitigated rancor—O God, that I
were a man! I would eat his heart in the market place.

271 **it**：the words of your oath.

272, 273 **it**：my sword，也就是说，以剑起誓。如果有人否认我爱你，我就要和他决斗。

275—276 **sauce**：调味汁（与上面所说的 eat 配成一譬喻，表示在任何情况下不会收回他的话）。　**to it**：to go with it.　**protest**：swear, solemnly affirm.

279 **stayed**：stopped.　**in … hour**：at a favorable moment.

287 **to deny it**：by refusing to do it.

288 **Tarry**：wait a minute.

289 **I … here**：Though my body is here，my heart has left here.

294 **dare easier**：are more courageous to.

297 **'a**：he.　**approved**：proved.　**height**：highest degree.

299 **bear her in hand**：lead her on.

300 **take hands**：join hands，marry.

301 **uncovered**：undisguised.　**rancor**：hatred.

BENEDICK   Hear me, Beatrice—

BEATRICE   Talk with a man out at a window! —a proper
305   saying!

BENEDICK   Nay, but Beatrice—

BEATRICE   Sweet Hero! she is wronged, she is slandered, she is undone.

BENEDICK   Beat—

310 BEATRICE   Princes and Counties! Surely a princely testimony, a goodly count, Count Comfect, a sweet gallant
surely! O that I were a man for his sake! or that I had
any friend would be a man for my sake! But manhood
is melted into cursies, valor into compliment, and men
315   are only turned into tongue, and trim ones too. He is
now as valiant as Hercules that only tells a lie, and
swears it. I cannot be a man with wishing; therefore I
will die a woman with grieving.

BENEDICK   Tarry, good Beatrice. By this hand, I love
thee.

320 BEATRICE   Use it for my love some other way than swea-
ring by it.

BENEDICK   Think you in your soul the Count Claudio hath
wronged Hero?

BEATRICE   Yea, as sure as I have a thought or a soul.

325 BENEDICK   Enough, I am engaged. I will challenge him. I
will kiss your hand, and so I leave you. By this hand,
Claudio shall render me a dear account. As you hear of
me, so think of me. Go comfort your cousin. I must
say she is dead — and so farewell.

                                    [*Exeunt*.]

308 **undone**：ruined.

310 **Counties**：counts.

311 **Count**：①伯爵（指 Claudio）；②叙述，故事；③ legal indictment，罪状。 **Comfect**：comfit, sweet containing nut.

314 **cursies**：curtsies. **compliment**：flattery.

315—316 **trim**：glib. **He … that**：the man who.

325 **engaged**：bound by a promise. **challenge him**：向他提出决斗。

327—328 **render … account**：give me a worthy account，向我作出像样的交代。 **As … me**：think of me according to the news you receive about me.

SCENE II

A hearing-room in Messina

*Enter the Constables [Dogberry and Verges]
and the Town Clerk [Sexton] in gowns, Borachio [, Conrade, and Watch].*

DOGBERRY Is our whole dissembly appeared?

VERGES O, a stool and a cushion for the sexton.

SEXTON Which be the malefactors?

DOGBERRY Marry, that am I and my partner.

5 VERGES Nay, that's certain. We have the exhibition to
examine.

SEXTON But which are the offenders that are to be examined? let them come before master constable.

DOGBERRY Yea, marry, let them come before me. What

10 is your name, friend?

BORACHIO Borachio.

DOGBERRY Pray write down Borachio. Yours, sirrah?

CONRADE I am a gentleman, sir, and my name is Conrade.

DOGBERRY Write down Master Gentleman Conrade.
Masters, do you serve God?

15 BOTH Yea, sir, we hope.

DOGBERRY Write down that they hope they serve God;
and write God first, for God defend but God should go
before such villains! Masters, it is proved already that
you are little better than false knaves, and it will go

20 near to be thought so shortly. How answer you for
yourselves?

CONRADE Marry, sir, we say we are none.

DOGBERRY A marvellous witty fellow, I assure you; but
I will go about with him. [*to Borachio*] Come you hith-

25 er, sirrah. A word in your ear. Sir, I say to you, it is

IV. ii

hearing-room：审讯室。

1 **dissembly**：a mistake for 'assembly'.

3 **malefactors**：evil-doers.

4 **Marry，… partner**：Dogberry 误以为 malefactors 是指审讯官。

5 **exhibition**：a mistake for 'commission' (order).

12 **sirrah?**：喂（招呼下级的词）。

14 **Master Gentleman**：绅士老爷。 **Masters**：大爷们。 **serve**：render obedience to.

17 **God defend but God should**：God forbid that God should not.

24 **go about with**：tackle with，get the better of.

thought you are false knaves.

BORACHIO   Sir, I say to you we are none.

DOGBERRY   Well, stand aside. Fore God, they are both
in a tale. Have you writ down that they are none?

30 SEXTON   Master constable, you go not the way to examine. You must call forth the watch that are their accus-
ers.

DOGBERRY   Yea, marry, that's the eftest way. Let the
watch come forth. Masters, I charge you in the
Prince's name accuse these men.

35 1. WATCH   This man said, sir, that Don John the Prince's
brother was a villain.

DOGBERRY   Write down Prince John a villain. Why, this
is flat perjury, to call a prince's brother villain.

BORACHIO   Master constable —

40 DOGBERRY   Pray thee, fellow, peace. I do not like thy
look, I promise thee.

SEXTON   What heard you him say else?

2. WATCH   Marry, that he had received a thousand ducats
of Don John for accusing the Lady Hero wrongfully.

45 DOGBERRY   Flat burglary as ever was committed.

VERGES   Yea, by mass, that it is.

SEXTON   What else, fellow?

1. WATCH   And that Count Claudio did mean, upon his
words, to disgrace Hero before the whole assembly, and
50 not marry her.

DOGBERRY   O villain! thou wilt be condemned into ever-
lasting redemption for this.

SEXTON   What else?

WATCHMEN   This is all.

55 SEXTON   And this is more, masters, than you can deny.
Prince John is this morning secretly stolen away. Hero
was in this manner accused, in this very manner refused, and upon the grief of this suddenly died. Master

28—29 **Fore**: before.　**are both in a tale**: both tell the same story.　**writ**: written.

30 **go not the way**: are not acting the proper way.

32 **eftest**: deftest, quickest (This is Dogberry's invention).

40 **peace**: silence.

45 **burglary**: 盗窃行为(Dogberry 显然又用错了字)。

46 **by mass**: by the mass (a common oath).

52 **redemption**: a mistake for 'damnation'.

56 **is … stolen away**: has gone away stealthily.

57—58 **refused**: cast off.　**upon**: from.

constable, let these men be bound and brought to Le-

60 onato's. I will go before and show him their examination. [*Exit.*]

DOGBERRY Come, let them be opinioned.

VERGES Let them be in the hands —

CONRADE Off, coxcomb!

DOGBERRY God's my life, where's the sexton? Let him

65 write down the Prince's officer coxcomb. Come, bind
them. — Thou naughty varlet!

CONRADE Away! you are an ass, you are an ass.

DOGBERRY Dost thou not suspect my place? Dost thou
not suspect my years? O that he were here to write me

70 down an ass! But, masters, remember that I am an
ass. Though it be not written down, yet forget not
that I am an ass. No, thou villain, thou art full of piety, as shall be proved upon thee by good witness. I am
a wise fellow; and which is more, an officer; and which

75 is more, a householder; and which is more, as pretty a
piece of flesh as any is in Messina, and one that knows
the law, go to! and a rich fellow enough, go to! and a
fellow that hath had losses; and one that hath two
gowns and everything handsome about him. Bring him

80 away. O that I had been writ down an ass!

Exit [*with the others*].

61   opinioned：a mistake for 'pinioned'.

63   coxcomb!：小丑（系由宫廷弄臣头上戴的红色法兰绒鸡冠帽 coxcomb 而得名）。

64   God's my life：是 God save my life 的缩写，一般指赌咒语。

66   naughty：wicked.   **varlet**：scoundrel.

69   suspect：a mistake for 'respect'.

72—73   piety：a mistake for 'impiety'.

74   which：what.

75—76   as … as any：as handsome a man as any.

77   go to!：去你的!

78—79   hath had losses：implying that he was once even richer.
gowns：cloaks trimmed with fur or velvet.

ACT V

SCENE I

A Street in Messina

Enter Leonato and his brother [Antonio].

ANTONIO

If you go on thus, you will kill yourself,
And 'tis not wisdom thus to second grief
Against yourself.

LEONATO   I pray thee cease thy counsel,
Which falls into mine ears as profitless

5   As water in a sieve. Give not me counsel,
Nor let no comforter delight mine ear
But such a one whose wrongs do suit with mine.
Bring me a father that so loved his child,
Whose joy of her is overwhelmed like mine,

10   And bid him speak of patience.
Measure his woe the length and breadth of mine,
And let it answer every strain for strain,
As thus for thus, and such a grief for such,
In every lineament, branch, shape, and form.

15   If such a one will smile and stroke his beard,
Bid sorrow wag, cry 'hem' when he should groan,
Patch grief with proverbs, make misfortune drunk
With candle-wasters—bring him yet to me,
And I of him will gather patience.

20   But there is no such man; for, brother, men
Can counsel and speak comfort to that grief
Which they themselves not feel; but, tasting it,
Their counsel turns to passion, which before

V. i

    2 **second**：support；assist.

    7 **suit with**：match.

    9 **overwhelmed**：crushed or overcome completely and suddenly.

    11 **Measure his woe**：ascertain his woe by comparison with.

    12 **let … strain**：let his woe return trait for trait（answer strain for strain 又可解 echo tune for tune）.

    16 **wag**：go away. **cry 'hem'**：cough lightly（in hesitation or doubt）.

    17—18 **make … candle-wasters**：drown grief with the wise sayings of moral philosophers. **candle-wasters**：burners of midnight oil. **yet**：now as always.

    19 **of him**：from him.

    22 **Which**：其先行词为 counsel.

Would give preceptial medicine to rage,
25 Fetter strong madness in a silken thread,
Charm ache with air and agony with words.
No, no! 'Tis all men's office to speak patience
To those that wring under the load of sorrow,
But no man's virtue nor sufficiency
30 To be so moral when he shall endure
The like himself. Therefore give me no counsel.
My griefs cry louder than advertisement.

ANTONIO

Therein do men from children nothing differ.

LEONATO

I pray thee peace. I will be flesh and blood;
35 For there was never yet philosopher
That could endure the toothache patiently,
However they have writ the style of gods
And made a push at chance and sufferance.

ANTONIO

Yet bend not all the harm upon yourself.
40 Make those that do offend you suffer too.

LEONATO

There thou speak'st reason. Nay, I will do so.
My soul doth tell me Hero is belied;
And that shall Claudio know; so shall the Prince,
And all of them that thus dishonor her.

Enter Prince [*Don Pedro*] *and Claudio.*

ANTONIO

45 Here comes the Prince and Claudio hastily.

PEDRO

Good den, good den.

CLAUDIO   Good day to both of you.

LEONATO

Hear you, my lords—

PEDRO   We have some haste, Leonato.

24 **preceptial medicine**：medicine in the form of precepts. **rage** (n.)：violent emotion.

25 **in**：with.

26 **Charm**：appease；allay.

27 **office**：business.

28 **wring** (v. i.)：writhe；suffer torture.

29 **sufficiency**：ability.

30 **moral**：full of moral precepts；moralistic.

31 **The like**：similar things.

32 **advertisement**：advice. 此句说 my grief is too great to be consoled by advice.

33 **Therein … differ**：in other words, you are being childish.

37 **writ … gods**：written in a style of god-like superiority.

38 **made … sufferance**：scoffed at misfortune and suffering.

39 **bend**：turn.

42 **belied**：slandered.

45 **comes**：先行(故用单数,这是当时一种特殊用法)。

46 **Good den**：good evening.

47 **have some haste**：are in haste.

LEONATO

 Some haste, my lord! well, fare you well, my lord.
 Are you so hasty now? Well, all is one.

PEDRO

50 Nay, do not quarrel with us, good old man.

ANTONIO

 If he could right himself with quarrelling,
 Some of us would lie low.

CLAUDIO   Who wrongs him?

LEONATO

 Marry, thou dost wrong me, thou dissembler, thou!
 Nay, never lay thy hand upon thy sword;
 I fear thee not.

55 CLAUDIO   Marry, beshrew my hand

 If it should give your age such cause of fear.
 In faith, my hand meant nothing to my sword.

LEONATO

 Tush, tush, man! never fleer and jest at me.
 I speak not like a dotard nor a fool,

60 As under privilege of age to brag
 What I have done being young, or what would do,
 Were I not old. Know, Claudio, to thy head,
 Thou hast so wronged mine innocent child and me
 That I am forced to lay my reverence by

65 And, with grey hairs and bruise of many days,
 Do challenge thee to trial of a man.
 I say thou hast belied mine innocent child.
 Thy slander hath gone through and through her heart,
 And she lies buried with her ancestors—

70 O, in a tomb where never scandal slept,
 Save this of hers, framed by thy villainy!

CLAUDIO

 My villainy?

LEONATO   Thine, Claudio; thine I say.

49   **all is one**: it does not matter.

51   **right himself**: avenge the wrong done him.

52   **Some of us**: 指 Claudio 和 Pedro.   **lie low**: lie dead.

53   **thou!**: Leonato 对 Claudio 改称 thou，是敌意的表示。

55   **beshrew**: a curse on; plague on (mild curse).

57   **to**: in moving to.

58   **fleer**: jeer, sneer.

62   **Know, ... to thy head**: I am telling you to your face.

64   **lay my reverence by**: lay aside the dignity of my old age.

65   **bruise**: wear and tear,经受的风霜。

66   **trial of a man**: manly test, i. e., a duel.

67   **belied**: told lies about.

71   **framed**: made.

PEDRO

    You say not right, old man.

LEONATO   My lord, my lord.

    I'll prove it on his body if he dare,

75   Despite his nice fence and his active practice,

    His May of youth and bloom of lustihood.

CLAUDIO

    Away! I will not have to do with you.

LEONATO

    Canst thou so daff me? Thou hast killed my child.

    If thou kill'st me, boy, thou shalt kill a man.

ANTONIO

80   He shall kill two of us, and men indeed.

    But that's no matter; let him kill one first.

    Win me and wear me! Let him answer me.

    Come, follow me, boy. Come, sir boy, come follow me.

    Sir boy, I'll whip you from your foining fence!

85   Nay, as I am a gentleman, I will.

LEONATO

    Brother —

ANTONIO

    Content yourself. God knows I loved my niece,

    And she is dead, slandered to death by villains,

    That dare as well answer a man indeed

90   As I dare take a serpent by the tongue.

    Boys, apes, braggarts, Jacks, milksops!

LEONATO   Brother Anthony—

ANTONIO

    Hold you content. What, man! I know them, yea,

    And what they weigh, even to the utmost scruple,

    Scambling, outfacing, fashion-monging boys,

95   That lie and cog and flout, deprave and slander,

    Go anticly, show outward hideousness,

    And speak off half a dozen dang'rous words,

74 **on his body**：by killing him in a duel.

75 **nice fence**：skilful fencing.

76 **lustihood**：vigour, strength.

77 **have to do**：have anything to do.

78 **daff me**：put me off.

79 **man**：大丈夫。

81 **no matter**：not important.

82 **Win … me!**：a proverbial way of challenge meaning. 'Let him overcome me, and he is welcome to boast'.

83 **boy**：小子(表示轻蔑)。

84 **foining**：thrusting (a fencing term).

87 **Content**：calm.

89 **as well**：此处等于 as little. **answer a man**：take up a man's challenge to a duel.

91 **apes**：fools. **Jacks**：knaves. **Anthony**：Antonio 的英语拼法。

92 **Hold you content**：keep calm.

93 **scruple**：smallest measure of weight.

94 **Scambling**：scrambling. **outfacing**：impudent. **fashion-mong-ing**：fashion-mongering, foppish.

95 **cog**：cheat. **flout**：mock, jeer. **deprave**：defame.

96 **Go anticly**：act grotesquely. **outward hideousness**：hideous appearance.

How they might hurt their enemies, if they durst;
And this is all.

LEONATO

But, brother Anthony —

100   ANTONIO   Come, 'tis no matter.
Do not you meddle; let me deal in this.

PEDRO

Gentlemen both, we will not wake your patience.
My heart is sorry for your daughter's death;
But, on my honor, she was charged with nothing

105   But what was true, and very full of proof.

LEONATO

My lord, my lord —

PEDRO

I will not hear you.

LEONATO

No? Come, brother, away! — I will be heard.

ANTONIO

And shall, or some of us will smart for it.

Exeunt ambo. Enter Benedick.

110   PEDRO See, see! Here comes the man we went to seek.

CLAUDIO Now, signior, what news?

BENEDICK Good day, my lord.

PEDRO Welcome, signior. You are almost come to part
almost a fray.

115   CLAUDIO We had liked to have had our two noses
snapped off with two old men without teeth.

PEDRO Leonato and his brother. What think'st thou?
Had we fought, I doubt we should have been too young
for them.

120   BENEDICK In a false quarrel there is no true valor. I came
to seek you both.

CLAUDIO We have been up and down to seek thee; for we
are high-proof melancholy, and would fain have it beat-
en away. Wilt thou use thy wit?

102   **wake**：arouse，excite.

105   **full of proof**：fully proved.

109   **shall**：you shall be heard（shall 用于第二人称表命令）。
or：otherwise.   **smart**：suffer great pain.

ambo〈拉丁语〉：both.

113   **almost come**：come almost in time.   **part**：separate.

115   **We had liked**：we were likely.

116   **with**：by.

118   **doubt**：suspect.

123—124   **high-proof**：in a high degree of.   **fain**：willingly.
beaten away：dispelled.

125　BENEDICK　It is in my scabbard. Shall I draw it?

　　　PEDRO　Dost thou wear thy wit by thy side?

　　　CLAUDIO　Never any did so, though very many have been
　　　　beside their wit. I will bid thee draw, as we do the
　　　　minstrels — draw to pleasure us.

130　PEDRO　As I am an honest man, he looks pale. Art thou
　　　　sick, or angry?

　　　　CLAUDIO　What, courage, man! What though care
　　　　killed a cat, thou hast mettle enough in thee to kill
　　　　care.

　　　BENEDICK　Sir, I shall meet your wit in the career an you
135　　charge it against me. I pray you choose another sub-
　　　　ject.

　　　CLAUDIO　Nay then, give him another staff; this last was
　　　　broke cross.

　　　PEDRO　By this light, he changes more and more. I think
　　　　he be angry indeed.

140　CLAUDIO　If he be, he knows how to turn his girdle.

　　　BENEDICK　Shall I speak a word in your ear?

　　　CLAUDIO　God bless me from a challenge!

　　　BENEDICK　[*aside to Claudio*] You are a villain. I jest not;
　　　　I will make it good how you dare, with what you
145　　dare, and when you dare. Do me right, or I will pro-
　　　　test your cowardice. You have killed a sweet lady, and
　　　　her death shall fall heavy on you. Let me hear from
　　　　you.

　　　　CLAUDIO　Well, I will meet you, so I may have good
　　　　cheer.

　　　PEDRO　What, a feast? a feast?

150　CLAUDIO　I' faith, I thank him, he hath bid me to a
　　　　calve's head and a capon, the which if I do not carve
　　　　most curiously, say my knife's naught. Shall I not find
　　　　a woodcock too?

　　　BENEDICK　Sir, your wit ambles well; it goes easily.

125 **it**：①wit；②sword.

128 **beside their wit**：beside themselves，out of their minds. **draw**：draw the bow across a fiddle. Claudio does not realize that Benedick is serious.

129 **pleasure**：please.

130 **As … man**：as sure as I am an honest man，凭我的诚实作证。

132—133 **care … cat**：(谚语)"忧虑伤身"，因 a cat has nine lives.

133 **mettle**：fiery temper.

134 **in the career**：at full charge. career 指持矛比武中 a short gallop at full speed.   **an**：if，下同。

136 **staff**：lance，矛。

137 **broke**：broken.

138 **By this light**：by God's light，by heaven，天哪。

139 **be**：虚拟语气,在宾语从句中表猜想。

140 **turn his girdle**：忍气吞声,(谚语) 'If you be angry，you may turn the buckle of your girdle behind you.'

142 **bless**：preserve.

144 **make it good**：back up my word by fighting. **how you dare**：in any way you dare fight.   **with what**：with any weapon.

145—146 **Do me right**：give me satisfaction. **protest**：proclaim.

147 **hear from you**：have your answer.

148 **cheer**：双关语 1. mirth，entertainment；2. food.

150—151 **bid**：invited.   **calve**：双关语 1. calf；2. fool.

151—152 **capon**：双关语 1. chicken；2. weakling. **curiously**：expertly，skilfully.

152—153 **naught**：good for nothing. **woodcock**：双关语 1. 山鹬；2. simpleton.

154 **ambles**：moves easily.

155 PEDRO I'll tell thee how Beatrice praised thy wit the
other day. I said thou hadst a fine wit: 'True,' said
she, 'a fine little one.' 'No,' said I, 'a great wit.'
'Right,' says she, 'a great gross one.' 'Nay,' said
I, 'a good wit.' 'Just,' said she, 'it hurts nobody.'

160 'Nay,' said I, 'the gentleman is wise.' 'Certain,' said
she, 'a wise gentleman,' 'Nay', said I, 'he hath the
tongues.' 'That I believe,' said she, 'for he swore a
thing to me on Monday night which he forswore on
Tuesday morning. There's a double tongue; there's

165 two tongues.' Thus did she an hour together transshape
thy particular virtues. Yet at last she concluded with a
sigh, thou wast the properest man in Italy.

CLAUDIO For the which she wept heartily and said she
cared not.

PEDRO Yea, that she did; but yet for all that, an if she
170 did not hate him deadly, she would love him dearly.
The old man's daughter told us all.

CLAUDIO All, all! and moreover, God saw him when he
was hid in the garden.

PEDRO But when shall we set the savage bull's horns on
175 the sensible Benedick's head?

CLAUDIO Yea, and text underneath, 'Here dwells Benedick, the married man'?

BENEDICK Fare you well, boy; you know my mind. I
will leave you now to your gossip-like humor. You
180 break jests as braggarts do their blades, which God
be thanked hurt not. [*to the Prince*] My lord, for
your many courtesies I thank you. I must discontinue your company. Your brother the bastard is
fled from Messina. You have among you killed a
185 sweet and innocent lady. For my Lord Lackbeard
there, he and I shall meet; and till then peace be with
him. [*Exit.*]

155 **praised**：appraised，评价。

156，157 **fine**：前者 excellent，后者 small.

158—159 **gross**：vulgar, stupid.　**Just**：correct.

161—162 **wise gentleman**：wiseacre，自作聪明的人。　　**hath the tongues**：speak several languages.

165 **transshape**：transform.

166 **particular**：personal.

167 **properest**：most handsome.

169 **an if**：if.

171 **The old man's daughter**：指 Hero，见 3 幕 1 场。

172—173 **God … garden**：《圣经·旧约·创世记》第 3 章 8 节，上帝看到吃禁果后的亚当想在伊甸园里躲起来，但也指 Benedick 藏在藤架后偷听的事。

174 **savage bull's horns**：见 I. i 245—251 行。

176 **text**：caption.

179 **gossip-like**：tattling.　**humor**：mood.

180 **break jests**：crack jokes.

182—183 **discontinue your company**：leave you.

183—184 **is fled**：has fled.

186 **meet**：meet in duel.

PEDRO   He is in earnest.

CLAUDIO   In most profound earnest; and, I'll warrant
you, for the love of Beatrice.

190   PEDRO   And hath challenged thee?

CLAUDIO   Most sincerely.

PEDRO   What a pretty thing man is when he goes in his
doublet and hose and leaves off his wit!

> *Enter Constables* [*Dogberry and Verges, with*
> *the Watch, leading*] *Conrade and Borachio.*

CLAUDIO   He is then a giant to an ape; but then is an ape
195   a doctor to such a man.

PEDRO   But, soft you, let me be! Pluck up, my heart,
and be sad! Did he not say my brother was fled?

DOGBERRY   Come you, sir. If justice cannot tame you,
she shall ne'er weigh more reasons in her balance.
200   Nay, an you be a cursing hypocrite once, you must be
looked to.

PEDRO   How now? two of my brother's men bound? Borachio one.

CLAUDIO   Hearken after their offense, my lord.

PEDRO   Officers, what offense have these men done?

205   DOGBERRY   Marry, sir, they have committed false report; moreover, they have spoken untruths; secondarily, they are slanders; sixth and lastly, they have belied
a lady; thirdly, they have verified unjust things; and to
conclude, they are lying knaves.

210   PEDRO   First, I ask thee what they have done; thirdly, I
ask thee what's their offense; sixth and lastly, why
they are committed; and to conclude, what you lay to
their charge.

CLAUDIO   Rightly reasoned, and in his own division; and
215   by my troth there's one meaning well suited.

PEDRO   Who have you offended, masters, that you are
thus bound to your answer? This learned constable is

192—193 pretty：fine(反话)。 **goes in his doublet and hose**：脱去长外衣，只穿上衣和紧身裤，是准备决斗的装束。

194—195 He … man：He then seems to be much bigger than an ape (a fool), but the ape is much wiser than he.

195 doctor：learned man.

196 soft：stay, stop.

197 sad：serious.

198 justice：司正义的女神手执天平(balance)，衡量是非。

199 reasons：除作为理由解外，当时读音和 raisins(葡萄干)一样，故有开玩笑之义。

200 an：if. **looked to**：guarded.

203 Hearken after：inquire into.

207 slanders：slanderers. **belied**：slandered.

208 verified：sworn to.

212 committed：arrested and held for trial.

214 division：dividing into categories.

215 well suited：provided with several different suits, or modes of speech.

217 bound：双关语 1. 被捆绑；2. 被勒令。 **to your answer**：对你的行为作出解释。

too cunning to be understood. What's your offense?

BORACHIO Sweet Prince, let me go no farther to mine
220 answer. Do you hear me, and let this Count kill me. I
have deceived even your very eyes. What your wisdoms
could not discover, these shallow fools have brought to
light, who in the night overheard me confessing to this
man, how Don John your brother incensed me to
225 slander the Lady Hero; how you were brought into the
orchard and saw me court Margaret in Hero's garments; how you disgraced her when you should
marry her. My villainy they have upon record, with
I had rather seal with my death than repeat over to my
230 shame. The lady is dead upon mine and my master's
false accusation; and briefly, I desire nothing but the
reward of a villain.

PEDRO Runs not this speech like iron through your blood? .

CLAUDIO I have drunk poison whiles he uttered it.

235 PEDRO But did my brother set thee on to this?

BORACHIO Yea, and paid me richly for the practice of it.

PEDRO

He is composed and framed of treachery,

And fled he is upon this villainy.

CLAUDIO

Sweet Hero, now thy image doth appear
240 In the rare semblance that I loved it first.

DOGBERRY Come, bring away the plaintiffs. By this time
our sexton hath reformed Signior Leonato of the matter. And, masters, do not forget to specify, when time
and place shall serve, that I am an ass.

245 VERGES Here, here comes Master Signior Leonato, and
the sexton too.

Enter Leonato, his brother [Antonio], and the
Sexton.

218 **cunning**: clever.

224 **incensed**: incited.

229 **over**: from beginning to end.

233 **iron**: a sword.

236 **practice**: carrying out.

240 **rare semblance**: exceptional beauty.

241 **plaintiffs**: a mistake for 'defendants'.

242 **reformed**: a mistake for 'informed'.

243 **specify**: mention specifically.

LEONATO

    Which is the villain? Let me see his eyes,

    That, when I note another man like him,

    I may avoid him. Which of these is he?

BORACHIO

    If you would know your wronger, look on me.

LEONATO

250   Art thou the slave that with thy breath hast killed

    Mine innocent child?

BORACHIO   Yea, even I alone.

LEONATO

    No, not so, villain! thou beliest thyself.

    Here stand a pair of honorable men —

    A third is fled — that had a hand in it.

255   I thank you princes for my daughter's death.

    Record it with your high and worthy deeds.

    'Twas bravely done, if you bethink you of it.

CLAUDIO

    I know not how to pray your patience;

    Yet I must speak. Choose your revenge yourself;

260   Impose me to what penance your invention

    Can lay upon my sin. Yet sinned I not

    But in mistaking.

PEDRO   By my soul, nor I!

    And yet, to satisfy this good old man,

    I would bend under any heavy weight

265   That he'll enjoin me to.

LEONATO

    I cannot bid you bid my daughter live —

    That were impossible; but I pray you both,

    Possess the people in Messina here

    How innocent she died; and if your love

270   Can labor aught in sad invention,

    Hang her an epitaph upon her tomb,

247 **That**: so that.

257 **bethink you of**: recall.

258 **pray your patience**: ask your forgiveness.

260 **Impose**: subject. **invention**: imagination.

261—262 **not/But**: only.

262 **mistaking**: mistake.

267 **were**: would be.

268 **Possess**: inform.

270 **labor aught**: work out anything. **invention**: poetic skill.

And sing it to her bones — sing it to-night.
To-morrow morning come you to my house,
And since you could not be my son-in-law,
275   Be yet my nephew. My brother hath a daughter,
Almost the copy of my child that's dead,
And she alone is heir to both of us.
Give her the right you should have giv'n her cousin,
And so dies my revenge.

CLAUDIO   O noble sir!
280   Your over-kindness doth wring tears from me.
I do embrace your offer; and dispose
For henceforth of poor Claudio.

LEONATO

To-morrow then I will expect your coming;
To-night I take my leave. This naughty man
285   Shall face to face be brought to Margaret,
Who I believe was packed in all this wrong,
Hired to it by your brother.

BORACHIO   No, by my soul, she was not;
Nor knew not what she did when she spoke to me;
But always hath been just and virtuous
290   In anything that I do know by her.

DOGBERRY Moreover, sir, which indeed is not under
white and black, this plaintiff here, the offender, did
call me ass. I beseech you let it be remembered in his
punishment. And also the watch heard them talk of one
295   Deformed. They say he wears a key in his ear, and a
lock hanging by it, and borrows money in God's
name, the which he hath used so long and never paid
that now men grow hardhearted and will lend nothing
for God's sake. Pray you examine him upon that point.
300   LEONATO I thank thee for thy care and honest pains.

DOGBERRY Your worship speaks like a most thankful and
reverent youth, and I praise God for you.

278 **right**: right of becoming your wife (perhaps with pun on 'rite' of marriage).

281 **dispose**: you may dispose.

284 **naughty**: wicked.

286 **packed**: involved as an accomplice.

289 **just**: honorable.

290 **by**: of.

291—292 **under white and black**: in writing. **plaintiff**: a mistake for 'defendant'.

295—296 **key… lock**: his misunderstanding of the lock (发绺) or III. iii 157 行。

LEONATO There's for thy pains.

   [*Gives money.*]

DOGBERRY God save the foundation!

305 LEONATO Go, I discharge thee of thy prisoner, and I
thank thee.

DOGBERRY I leave an arrant knave with your worship,
which I beseech your worship to correct yourself, for
the example of others. God keep your worship! I wish

310 your worship well. God restore you to health! I hum-
bly give you leave to depart; and if a merry meeting
may be wished, God prohibit it! Come, neighbor.

       Exeunt Dogberry and Verges.

LEONATO

Until to-morrow morning, lords, farewell.

ANTONIO

Farewell, my lords. We look for you to-morrow.

PEDRO

315 We will not fail.

CLAUDIO   To-night I'll mourn with Hero.

      Exeunt Don Pedro and Claudio.

LEONATO [*to the Watch*]

Bring you these fellows on. —We'll talk with Margaret,
How her acquaintance grew with this lewd fellow.

         Exeunt.

SCENE II

In front of Leonato's house

Enter Benedick and Margaret [*meeting*].

BENEDICK Pray thee, sweet Mistress Margaret, deserve
well at my hands by helping me to the speech of Beatrice.

MARGARET Will you then write me a sonnet in praise of

304　**foundation**：慈善基金会。　　**God … foundation!**：乞丐在接受施舍时常用的话，但在此并不合适。

305　**discharge**：relieve.

307　**arrant knave**：罪大恶极的坏蛋。

308　**which**：who（当时这两个词有时换用）。　　**correct yourself**：您亲自惩办。

311　**give you leave**：a mistake for 'ask your leave'.

312　**prohibit**：a mistake for 'grant'.

316　**mourn with**：mourn for.

318　**lewd**：base，low.

V. ii

1　**Mistress**：小姐（用于姓名前作称呼）。

my beauty?

5 BENEDICK In so high a style, Margaret, that no man living shall come over it; for in most comely truth thou
deservest it.

MARGARET To have no man come over me? Why, shall I
always keep below stairs?

10 BENEDICK Thy wit is as quick as the greyhound's mouth
— it catches.

MARGARET And yours's as blunt as the fencer's foils,
which hit but hurt not.

BENEDICK A most manly wit, Margaret: it will not hurt
a woman. And so I pray thee call Beatrice. I give thee
15 the bucklers.

MARGARET Give us the swords; we have bucklers of our
own.

BENEDICK If you use them, Margaret, you must put in
the pikes with a vice, and they are dangerous weapons
20 for maids.

MARGARET Well, I will call Beatrice to you, who I think
hath legs.   *Exit Margaret.*

BENEDICK And therefore will come.

[*Sings*] The god of love,
25   That sits above
And knows me, and knows me,
How pitiful I deserve —

I mean in singing; but in loving, Leander the good
swimmer, Troilus the first employer of panders, and
30 a whole book full of these quondam carpetmongers,
whose names yet run smoothly in the even road of a
blank verse — why, they were never so truly turned
over and over as my poor self in love. Marry, I cannot
show it in rhyme. I have tried. I can find out no rhyme
35 to 'lady' but 'baby' — an innocent rhyme; for
'scorn', 'horn' — a hard rhyme; for 'school', 'fool'

5 style：双关语 1. style of writing；2. stile,围栏上的梯级。

6 come over：surpass.

8 come over me?：lie on me.

9 keep below stairs?：live in the servants' rooms (which are below stairs) and never be mistress of a house.

10 catches：snatches.

11 foils：钝头剑。

13 manly：gentlemanly.

14—15 bucklers：中间安有长尖钉(spikes, pikes)的圆盾。 **I ... bucklers**：I surrender.

19 vice：screw.

27 I deserve：I am.

28 Leander：希腊神话中 Hero 的情人,每夜游过海峡去幽会,最后溺死。

29 Troilus：荷马史诗中 Troy 城邦王子之一,和希腊女子 Cressida 相爱,经她的叔父 Pandarus 相助私通。 **panders**：(淫乱之事的)拉皮条者,从 Pandarus 变来。

30 quondam〈拉丁语〉：formerly. **carpetmongers**：carpet knights, who have distinguished themselves on the carpet and not on the field of battle.

32—33 turned over and over：head over heels.

35 innocent：childish.

— a babbling rhyme. Very ominous endings! No, I was not born under a rhyming planet, nor I cannot woo in festival terms.

Enter Beatrice.

Sweet Beatrice, wouldst thou come when I called thee?

40 BEATRICE   Yea, signior, and depart when you bid me.

BENEDICK   O, stay but till then!

BEATRICE   'Then' is spoken. Fare you well now. And yet, ere I go, let me go with that I came for, which is, with knowing what hath passed between you and Claudio.

45 BENEDICK   Only foul words; and thereupon I will kiss thee.

BEATRICE   Foul words is but foul wind, and foul wind is but foul breath, and foul breath is noisome. Therefore I will depart unkissed.

BENEDICK   Thou hast frighted the word out of his right

50 sense, so forcible is thy wit. But I must tell thee plainly, Claudio undergoes my challenge; and either I must shortly hear from him or I will subscribe him a coward. And I pray thee now tell me, for which of my bad parts didst thou first fall in love with me?

55 BEATRICE   For them all together, which maintained so politic a state of evil that they will not admit any good part to intermingle with them. But for which of my good parts did you first suffer love for me?

BENEDICK   Suffer love! — a good epithet. I do suffer love

60 indeed, for I love thee against my will.

BEATRICE   In spite of your heart, I think. Alas, poor heart! If you spite it for my sake, I will spite it for yours, for I will never love that which my friend hates.

BENEDICK   Thou and I are too wise to woo peaceably.

65 BEATRICE   It appears not in this confession. There's not one wise man among twenty that will praise

38 **festival terms**：joyful words.

43 **that**：what.

45 **foul words**：strong language，恶言恶语。

47 **noisome**：offensive；bad-smelling.

49 **frighted**：frightened. **the word**：foul. **his**：its.

51 **undergoes**：bears；has received.

52 **subscribe him**：write him down；proclaim him.

53 **parts**：qualities.

56 **politic**：well-organized.

58 **suffer**：①experience；②feel the pain of.

59 **epithet**：expression.

61 **In spite of**：notwithstanding. 但 spite 也可解 ill-will，malice.

62 **spite**：vex，mortify.

himself.

BENEDICK An old, an old instance, Beatrice, that lived in
the time of good neighbors. If a man do not erect in
70   this age his own tomb ere he dies, he shall live no longer in monument than the bell rings and the widow
weeps.

BEATRICE And how long is that, think you?

BENEDICK Question: why, an hour in clamor and a quar-
75   ter in rheum. Therefore it is most expedient for
the wise, if Don Worm (his conscience) find no
impediment to the contrary, to be the trumpet of
his own virtues, as I am to myself. So much for
praising myself, who, I myself will bear witness, is
80   praiseworthy. And now tell me, how doth your cousin?

BEATRICE Very ill.

BENEDICK And how do you?

BEATRICE Very ill too.

85   BENEDICK Serve God, love me, and mend. There will I
leave you too, for here comes one in haste.

Enter Ursula.

URSULA Madam, you must come to your uncle. Yonder's old coil at home. It is proved my Lady Hero hath
90   been falsely accused, the Prince and Claudio mightily
abused, and Don John is the author of all, who is fled
and gone. Will you come presently?

BEATRICE Will you go hear this news, signior?

BENEDICK I will live in thy heart, die in thy lap, and be
95   buried in thy eyes; and moreover, I will go with thee to
thy uncle's.

Exit [with Beatrice and Ursula].

68 **instance**：proverb. **lived**：applied.

69 **time of good neighbors**：Golden Age. （谚语）'He who praises himself has ill neighbours'.

74 **Question**：Since you ask. **clamor**：audible cry.

75 **rheum**：tears.

76 **Don**〈西班牙语〉：先生。 **Worm**：alluding to the image of conscience as a tormenting 'worm'，见《圣经·以赛亚书》第 66 章 24 节,《圣经·新约·马可福音》第 9 章 48 节。

85 **and mend**：and you will recover your health.

89 **old**：great, abundant. **coil**：disturbance, noise, fuss.

90—91 **mightily**：greatly. **abused**：deceived. **author**：maker.

92 **presently**：immediately.

SCENE III

A Churchyard

Enter Claudio, Prince [Don Pedro, Lord],
and three or four with tapers [followed
by Musicians].

CLAUDIO Is this the monument of Leonato?
LORD It is, my lord.
CLAUDIO [*reads from a scroll*]
                    Epitaph.

        Done to death by slanderous tongues
            Was the Hero that here lies.
5   Death, in guerdon of her wrongs,
            Gives her fame which never dies.
        So the life that died with shame
        Lives in death with glorious fame.
            [*Hangs up the scroll.*]
        Hang thou there upon the tomb,
10   Praising her when I am dumb.
    Now, music, sound, and sing your solemn hymn.
                Song [by one attending].
        Pardon, goddess of the night,
        Those that slew thy virgin knight;
        For the which, with songs of woe,
15   Round about her tomb they go.
        Midnight, assist our moan,
        Help us to sigh and groan
            Heavily, heavily.
        Graves, yawn and yield your dead,
20   Till death be utterèd
            Heavily, heavily.
CLAUDIO Now unto thy bones good night!
        Yearly will I do this rite.

V. iii

    tapers：candles.

1   **monument of Leonato**：里奥那托家族的陵墓。

4   **Hero**：双关语 1. 希罗；2. 英雄。

5   **guerdon**：recompense.

12   **goddess of the night**：Diana.

13   **thy virgin knight**：Diana's virgin votary.

19   **yawn**：open.

20   **utter èd**：commemorated.

PEDRO

    Good morrow, masters. Put your torches out.

25   The wolves have preyed, and look, the gentle day,

    Before the wheels of Phoebus, round about

      Dapples the drowsy east with spots of grey.

    Thanks to you all, and leave us. Fare you well.

CLAUDIO

    Good morrow, masters. Each his several way.

PEDRO

30   Come, let us hence and put on other weeds,

      And then to Leonato's we will go.

CLAUDIO

    And Hymen now with luckier issue speed's

    Than this for whom we rend'red up this woe.

                      Exeunt.

SCENE IV

The hall in Leonato's house

Enter Leonato, Benedick, [Beatrice,] Margaret,
Ursula, Old Man [Antonio], Friar [Francis], Hero.

FRIAR

    Did I not tell you she was innocent?

LEONATO

    So are the Prince and Claudio, who accused her

    Upon the error that you heard debated.

    But Margaret was in some fault for this,

5   Although against her will, as it appears

    In the true course of all the question.

ANTONIO

    Well, I am glad that all things sort so well.

BENEDICK

    And so am I, being else by faith enforced

    To call young Claudio to a reckoning for it.

24   Good morrow：good morning.

26   Phoebus ['fiːbəs]：希腊神话中的太阳神，驾太阳车横过太空。

27   Dapples：variegates with patches (of light or color).

30   other weeds：clothes other than the mourning garb we have worn.

32   Hymen ['haimen]：希腊神话中婚姻之神。   **issue**：result. **speed's**：(may Hymen) speed us，bless us.

33   this：this person (Hero).

V. iv

3   Upon：because of.

5   against her will：unintentionally.

6   question：investigation.

7   sort：turn out.

8   faith：fidelity to my word.   **enforced**：forced；obliged.

LEONATO

10   Well, daughter, and you gentlewomen all,
Withdraw into a chamber by yourselves,
And when I send for you, come hither masked.
The Prince and Claudio promised by this hour
To visit me. You know your office, brother:

15   You must be father to your brother's daughter,
And give her to young Claudio.   *Exeunt Ladies.*

ANTONIO

Which I will do with confirmed countenance.

BENEDICK

Friar, I must entreat your pains, I think.

FRIAR

To do what, signior?

BENEDICK

20   To bind me, or undo me — one of them.
Signior Leonato, truth it is, good signior,
Your niece regards me with an eye of favor.

LEONATO

That eye my daughter lent her. 'Tis most true.

BENEDICK

And I do with an eye of love requite her.

LEONATO

25   The sight whereof I think you had from me,
From Claudio, and the Prince; but what's your will?

BENEDICK

Your answer, sir, is enigmatical;
But, for my will, my will is, your good will
May stand with ours, this day to be conjoined

30   In the state of honorable marriage;
In which, good friar, I shall desire your help.

LEONATO

My heart is with your liking.

FRIAR   And my help.

14   **office**：task.

17   **confirmed countenance**：composed face.

18   **entreat your pains**：ask for your help，beg to trouble you.

20   **bind**：双关语 1. bind to a wife；2. 捆起来。   **undo**：双关语 1. ruin；2. 解开。

28—29   **for**：as for.   **your … ours**：you may give your consent to our wish.   **stand with**：agree with.

Here comes the Prince and Claudio.

Enter Prince [Don Pedro] and Claudio and two
or three other.

PEDRO

Good morrow to this fair assembly.

LEONATO

35　Good morrow, Prince; good morrow, Claudio.

We here attend you. Are you yet determined

To-day to marry with my brother's daughter?

CLAUDIO

I'll hold my mind, were she an Ethiope.

LEONATO

Call her forth, brother. Here's the friar ready.

　　　　　　　　　　　　　　　[Exit Antonio.]

PEDRO

40　Good morrow, Benedick. Why, what's the matter

That you have such a February face,

So full of frost, of storm, and cloudiness?

CLAUDIO

I think he thinks upon the savage bull.

Tush, fear not, man! We'll tip thy horns with gold,

45　And all Europa shall rejoice at thee,

As once Europa did at lusty Jove

When he would play the noble beast in love.

BENEDICK

Bull Jove, sir, had an amiable low,

And some such strange bull leaped your father's cow

50　And got a calf in that same noble feat

Much like to you, for you have just his bleat.

Enter [Leonato's] brother [Antonio], Hero, Beatrice,
Margaret, Ursula [the ladies wearing masks].

CLAUDIO

For this I owe you. Here comes other reck'nings.

Which is the lady I must seize upon?

36 **attend**：wait for. **yet**：still.

38 **hold my mind**：keep to my intention. **Ethiope**：Ethiopian 通指黑皮肤的人（当时被认为是丑的）。

43 **bull**：见前 I. i 245 行和 V. i 174 行。

44 **tip**：cover the tip of.

45 **Europa**：Europe 因 Europa 而得名。

46 **Europa**：希腊罗马神话中天神 Jove 所垂爱，并化为白色公牛驮走的女郎。

48 **low**（n.）：牛叫声。

49 **leaped**：copulated with.

51 **like to**：like. **his**：its. **bleat**：牛叫声。

52 **I owe you**：I will pay you back（Benedick 既骂了他是私生子，又骂了他是牛崽子）。 **reck'nings**：matters to consider; obligations to fulfil.

ANTONIO

This same is she, and I do give you her.

CLAUDIO

55   Why then, she's mine. Sweet, let me see your face.

LEONATO

No, that you shall not till you take her hand

Before this friar and swear to marry her.

CLAUDIO

Give me your hand before this holy friar.

I am your husband if you like of me.

HERO

60   And when I lived I was your other wife;

          [*Unmasks.*]

And when you loved you were my other husband.

CLAUDIO

Another Hero!

HERO   Nothing certainer.

One Hero died defiled; but I do live,

And surely as I live, I am a maid.

PEDRO

65   The former Hero! Hero that is dead!

LEONATO

She died, my lord, but whiles her slander lived.

FRIAR

All this amazement can I qualify,

When, after that the holy rites are ended,

I'll tell you largely of fair Hero's death.

70   Meantime let wonder seem familiar,

And to the chapel let us presently.

BENEDICK

Soft and fair, friar. Which is Beatrice?

BEATRICE [*unmasks*]

I answer to that name. What is your will?

BENEDICK

59 **like of**：like.

63 **defiled**：disgraced（by the false charge）.

64 **surely as I live**：as sure as I live.

66 **but whiles**：only so long as.

67 **qualify**：moderate；relieve.

68 **after that**：after.

69 **largely**：in full；in detail.

70 **let ... familiar**：treat this wonderful happening as if it were an ordinary one.

72 **Soft and fair**：hold，stop（用于祈使语气中）。

Do not you love me?

BEATRICE   Why, no; no more than reason.

BENEDICK

75   Why, then your uncle, and the Prince, and Claudio
      Have been deceived — they swore you did.

BEATRICE

Do not you love me?

BENEDICK   Troth, no; no more than reason.

BEATRICE

Why, then my cousin, Margaret, and Ursula
Are much deceived; for they did swear you did.

BENEDICK

80   They swore that you were almost sick for me.

BEATRICE

They swore that you were well-nigh dead for me.

BENEDICK

'Tis no such matter. Then you do not love me?

BEATRICE

No, truly, but in friendly recompense.

LEONATO

Come, cousin, I am sure you love the gentleman.

CLAUDIO

85   And I'll be sworn upon't that he loves her;
      For here's a paper written in his hand,
      A halting sonnet of his own pure brain,
      Fashioned to Beatrice.

HERO   And here's another,

Writ in my cousin's hand, stol'n from her pocket,

90   Containing her affection unto Benedick.

BENEDICK A miracle! Here's our own hands against our
hearts. Come, I will have thee; but, by this light, I
take thee for pity.

BEATRICE I would not deny you; but, by this good day,
95   I yield upon great persuasion, and partly to save your

83   **but in friendly recompense**：except as a return of friendship.

87   **halting**：limping.

88   **Fashioned**：written.

91   **hands**：written testimony.

94   **deny**：refuse.   **by this good day**：I swear by this good day.（赌咒语）

95   **yield**：give way，not oppose.   **upon great persuasion**：being strongly urged（by friends）.

life, for I was told you were in a consumption.

BENEDICK Peace! I will stop your mouth.   [*Kisses her.*

PEDRO How dost thou, Benedick, the married man?

BENEDICK I'll tell thee what, Prince: a college of wit-
100   crackers cannot flout me out of my humor. Dost thou
think I care for a satire or an epigram? No. If a man
will be beaten with brains, 'a shall wear nothing handsome about him. In brief, since I do purpose to marry,
I will think nothing to any purpose that the world can
105   say against it; and therefore never flout at me for what
I have said against it; for man is a giddy thing, and this
is my conclusion. For thy part, Claudio, I did think to
have beaten thee; but in that thou art like to be my
kinsman, live unbruised, and love my cousin.

110 CLAUDIO I had well hoped thou wouldst have denied Beatrice, that I might have cudgelled thee out of thy single
life, to make thee a double-dealer, which out of question thou wilt be if my cousin do not look exceeding
narrowly to thee.

115 BENEDICK Come, come, we are friends. Let's have a
dance ere we are married, that we may lighten our own
hearts and our wives' heels.

LEONATO We'll have dancing afterward.

BENEDICK First, of my word! Therefore play, music.
120   Prince, thou art sad. Get thee a wife, get thee a wife!
There is no staff more reverent than one tipped with horn.

          Enter Messenger.

MESSENGER

My lord, your brother John is ta'en in flight,

And brought with arméd men back to Messina.

BENEDICK Think not on him till to-morrow. I'll devise
125   thee brave punishments for him. Strike up, pipers!

                              Dance [*Exeunt.*]

96   consumption: wasting disease.

99—100   college of wit-crackers: assembly of jokers.

100   flout: mock.   **humor**: inclination, idea.

101   care for: mind.   **epigram**: 讽刺小诗, 警句。

102—103   beaten with brains: defeated by witticisms.   **' a shall
… him**: he should not wear any finery — much less marry.

104   to any purpose: of any importance.

106   giddy: frivolous.

107   think to: intend to.

108   in that: since.   **like**: likely.

112   double-dealer: married man, but also an unfaithful husband
(a common newly-wed joke).

113—114   look exceeding narrowly to: watch most closely at.

119   of: upon.

121   staff: stick as sign of office or authority.   **tipped with horn**:
头上装了角(horn 影射绿帽子)。

124   on: of.

125   thee: an old dative 类似 for you.   **brave**: marvellous, excellent.   **Strike up**: begin playing.

图书在版编目(CIP)数据

无事生非／(英)莎士比亚(Shakespeare，W.)著；申恩荣注释.—北京：商务印书馆，2014(2016.3 重印)
(莎翁戏剧经典)
ISBN 978-7-100-09954-7

Ⅰ.①无… Ⅱ.①莎… ②申… Ⅲ.①英语—语言读物 ②剧本—英国—中世纪 Ⅳ.①H319.4：I

中国版本图书馆 CIP 数据核字(2013)第 095687 号

莎翁戏剧经典
WÚ SHÌ SHĒNG FĒI
无 事 生 非
〔英〕威廉·莎士比亚　著
申恩荣　注释

商 务 印 书 馆 出 版
(北京王府井大街36号　邮政编码 100710)
商 务 印 书 馆 发 行
北 京 冠 中 印 刷 厂 印 刷
ISBN 978-7-100-09954-7

2014 年 8 月第 1 版　　开本 787×1092　1/32
2016 年 3 月北京第 2 次印刷　印张 7　插页 1

定价：24.00 元